The New Handshake

Online Dispute Resolution and the Future of Consumer Protection

AMY J. SCHMITZ AND COLIN RULE

Cover design by Amanda Fry/ABA Design

Printed in the United States of America.

21 20 19 18 17 5 4 3 2 1

ISBN: 978-1-63425-767-1
e-ISBN: 978-1-63425-768-8

Library of Congress Cataloging-in-Publication Data

Names: Rule, Colin, author. | Schmitz, Amy J. (Law teacher), author. | American Bar Association. Section of Dispute Resolution, sponsoring body.
Title: Online dispute resolution and the future of consumer protection / Colin Rule and Amy J. Schmitz.
Description: Chicago : American Bar Association, 2017. | Includes bibliographical references and index.
Identifiers: LCCN 2016056080 (print) | LCCN 2016057621 (ebook) | ISBN 9781634257671 (softcover : alk. paper) | ISBN 9781634257688 (ebook)
Subjects: LCSH: Online dispute resolution—United States. | Consumer protection—Law and legislation—United States.
Classification: LCC KF9084 .R85 2017 (print) | LCC KF9084 (ebook) | DDC 343.7307/1—dc23
LC record available at https://lccn.loc.gov/2016056080

Discounts are available for books ordered in bulk. Special consideration is given to state bars, CLE programs, and other bar-related organizations. Inquire at Book Publishing, ABA Publishing, American Bar Association, 321 N. Clark Street, Chicago, Illinois 60654-7598.

www.shopABA.org

Dedication

Amy: for my Mom and Dad
Colin: for ABR and ADR

Contents

Foreword

Consumers International (CI), the world's largest federation of consumer groups, serves as the authoritative global voice for consumers. Since its founding on April 1, 1960, CI has grown to encompass more than 240 member organizations in 120 countries around the world. CI's goal is to build a powerful international movement to empower and protect consumers everywhere.

This global consumer movement is as diverse as it is far-reaching. Yet despite our differences, all CI members share a commitment to the promotion of eight core consumer rights—one of which is the right to redress. That right asserts that consumers should "receive a fair settlement of just claims, including compensation for misrepresentation, [for] shoddy goods or unsatisfactory services." The efforts of CI and its members during the last half-century have ensured that this right to redress is enshrined—alongside its companion rights—in the United Nation's *Guidelines on Consumer Protection* and in the consumer protection legislation of many countries around the world.

However, despite this progress, asserting that right and putting things right wherever they have gone wrong are still too difficult for consumers globally. The reality of seeking redress too often feels like trying to navigate a customer service labyrinth. We all know the frustration of being stuck at the end of a telephone, at our own expense, questioning the sincerity of the "your call is important to us" message as it interrupts the cycle of Muzak for the 53rd time.

This kind of frustrating experience is all too common when it comes to seeking redress. It can lead people to either abandon complaints at an early stage or even to abandon their attempts to seek redress in the first place, especially when the perceived opportunity cost of pursuing a complaint risks exceeding the value of the transaction that gave rise to the complaint. If the path to redress requires the consumer to initiate legal proceedings, many consumers are even less likely to attempt to secure a fair resolution.

Research in 2013 by the Ombudsman Services (UK) found that "40 million problems were not acted upon at all, as consumers choose to keep quiet." That silence keeps hidden a financial cost to consumers of unsatisfactory purchases that runs into hundreds of millions. When merchants and service providers view redress as a problem rather than a solution, consumers are left disempowered and this vital consumer right and protection is undermined. It should not be this way. The evidence shows consumers reward efficient and effective complaint resolution with increased loyalty and the feedback that complaints generate provides invaluable insights for companies, which can inform the changes needed to drive increased satisfaction.

The good news is that in an age where apps and web-based intermediary platforms are bringing convenience to every other aspect of the consumer experience and empowering consumers in dynamic new ways, we now have the means to apply the innovation, simplicity, and convenience that we have come to expect from our wider online experiences to our redress processes.

Although it is vital that we remember that access to the Internet and to connecting devices remains far from universal, we can at least observe this: Wherever access is widespread, the nature, the channel, and the timing of consumer transactions and interactions with providers of goods and services are being transformed for the better. Technology has brought consumers greater convenience, greater transparency, greater choice, and more information concerning those choices. The Internet in particular has given consumers voice in their interactions with business. The Internet also gives rise to a growing number of opportunities for fostering new forms of consumer empowerment and for enabling consumers to understand and assert their rights in more streamlined ways with more effective outcomes, with online dispute resolution (ODR) being a prime example.

We are only starting to see how the Internet will transform the consumer experience. The browser-based Internet that most consumers are familiar with is barely out of its teens. There is potential for technology to strike a significantly more equitable balance of power between the supply side and demand side of markets. Much of that potential resides in an emerging range of services that empower consumers to assert their rights and achieve their goals in convenient, dynamic ways.

ODR has the real potential to fit into this category. Effective ODR tools can take the friction out of complaining, thus making it much more likely a consumer will see a complaint through and get satisfaction. Additionally, ODR tools such as those offered by CI Members liberate the consumer from frustrations inherent in dealing with the customer services labyrinth, by providing an independent platform where consumer and supplier meet, and where the onus is placed on the vendor to respond.

The Internet provides new opportunities for collaboration between consumers, those who work on behalf of consumers, and merchants in this way. It is a new world where consumers' problems can be solved efficiently and effectively to the satisfaction of the consumer. That is why I am so enthusiastic about the *New Handshake*, because it offers a grand vision for how technology can be used to empower consumers and to provide fast and fair resolutions. The time is right to take advantage of new technology to build an accessible, transparent, scalable resolution system for both consumers and businesses. I hope the ideas in this book will spark conversations in board rooms, legislatures, and courthouses about how we can build new tools for providing consumers access to justice.

Amanda Long
Director General, Consumers International

Introduction

There was a time when merchants and consumers would meet in person to do business. They would discuss the terms, assess the trustworthiness and character of their contracting partners, and conclude the deal with a handshake. This handshake was more than a kind gesture. It helped to reassure both parties that the other side was committed to the deal and would ensure correction of any problems that might arise. Reputations and respect mattered most because individuals worked in the same community and knew each other's friends and business partners. That handshake sealed the deal. It was a personal trustmark.

Those days are gone. We rarely do deals on a handshake anymore. It is no longer realistic for us to insist upon face-to-face (F2F) meetings for all of our transactions in a digitized society. We text, Skype, FaceTime, and send e-mails. We cannot shake the other party's hand in person because so many of our transactions are now conducted online. Consumers increasingly turn to the Internet for their buying needs, both large and small. A physical handshake is simply impractical in these business-to-consumer (B2C) transactions. "Buying local" may be in vogue for farmers' markets and hip restaurants, but it is impractical for consumers shifting into the online world.

For consumers, e-commerce offers an enticing universe of possible connections. However, it also creates significant disconnections. There is little question that the Internet has become a gateway to an ever-expanding and globalized e-marketplace for consumer goods and services. It gives businesses access to multitudes of customers and introduces consumers to companies they would never otherwise encounter in the physical world. Nonetheless, the Internet has generated challenges for consumers as well by enabling some companies to easily hide from responsibility behind the anonymity and jurisdictional confusion of the Internet. Customer service representatives operating wholly online do not have to look customers in the eye when refusing to provide adequate remedies when purchases go awry. These anonymous representatives also may feel little to no loyalty to customers that are replaceable by a seemingly bottomless barrel of buyers unconstrained by geographic limitations.

The Internet also gives businesses an advantage in crafting and controlling the terms of consumer contracts. Businesses have access to reams of information across millions of transactions, and they have the power to set the terms of the exchange and insert their own fine print. They know that consumers do not read contracts. This is especially true when they are purchasing online. Some unscrupulous merchants can use this information and experience to their advantage, perhaps leading their buyers toward resolutions that are less advantageous, or even delaying events beyond filing windows to ensure the buyers lose their eligibility to register a claim.

As repeat players, merchants also enjoy an advantage in understanding all the precedent, policies, and procedural wrinkles in the systems they use to resolve issues with their buyers. Merchants may encounter hundreds, if not thousands, of disputes every month. They go through the resolution process over and over again, and they learn the ins and outs of typical and atypical cases. Consumers, on the other hand, probably encounter a resolution process once or twice every couple of years. Furthermore, when businesses unilaterally select redress processes such as arbitration, consumers rarely have any say in how the process works or any assurance that their interests will be protected.

These issues are further compounded because merchants are often reluctant to talk about the possibility of eventual problems at the time of the transaction. Merchants may fear that inklings of potential problems will dissuade buyers from completing their purchases. Furthermore, when a problem does eventually arise, information about contractually prescribed resolution processes may be buried in the fine print. Some businesses may also require complex procedural steps in order to dissuade consumers from pursuing redress. Also, merchants may be prone to appease the small number of customers who are determined enough to proactively seek redress in order to quiet these complainers without fixing the fundamental problems. This leaves a much larger pool of silent sufferers who are uninformed and unsatisfied.

In spite of these challenges, the Internet offers many structural advantages to consumers. The Internet enables consumers to share information in unprecedented ways. Consumers increasingly air their complaints on social media and review websites, helping other consumers identify bad actors so that other buyers can shop elsewhere. Suddenly, businesses have a huge stake in improving and protecting their reputations online. If consumers besmirch a business with a bad review, it may seriously harm that business's future prospects. Having a good reputation is now viewed as an essential asset that online merchants must carefully safeguard. Businesses that are successful in improving and protecting their reputations are the ones who grow and succeed.

This creates a strong incentive for merchants to be proactive about resolving buyer problems. If a business does not address difficulties encountered by their customers, word spreads quickly online. This puts buyers and sellers on the same side when it comes to quickly and effectively solving problems. Online platforms truly shine when they enable buyers and sellers to communicate and collaborate on an unprecedented scale. Whenever an issue arises, the buyer can immediately reach out to the seller and begin an online communication focused on getting the problem addressed. When parties reach a solution, they can immediately close the dispute and move on to the next transaction. This kind of instant collaboration, unconstrained by time and geography, would not be possible without the Internet.

In the past, debates about consumer protection have seemed zero-sum, with any advantage on one side seemingly connected to an equivalent disadvantage on the other. Business and consumer advocates have felt that they have little common ground. Wise businesses, however, now realize that building fast and fair consumer redress is extremely important for growing their customer base. In-depth analysis of large data sets in e-commerce demonstrates that effective resolution systems are enormously beneficial to businesses because they reduce costs of customer support and legal liability, while at the same time increasing customer loyalty. This means that the long-term economic benefits of effective resolution programs far outweigh the short-term costs associated with the programs' implementation.

The time is thus ripe for a new approach to consumer redress: one that addresses the shortcomings in current consumer protection systems and revives the sense of responsibility that underscored the "old handshake" of yore. We must leverage the power of the Internet to expand and equalize access to consumer redress. Fortunately, we have a model for how to achieve this. It is called online dispute resolution (ODR), and it marries information and communications technologies to the offline processes of negotiation, mediation, and arbitration—opening the door to a *New Handshake* for the Internet age.

This *New Handshake* is especially needed for the resolution of low-dollar claims, such as those in most B2C contexts. Consumers will inevitably lose trust in online marketplaces that lack reasonable remedy systems for these claims. ODR creates new hope for these consumers by operating swiftly and independently of the courts, eliminating procedural complexities and choice of law concerns. Furthermore, resolution processes can be integrated directly into the websites where transactions take place. ODR systems lower the costs and burdens of pursuing purchase complaints. Consumers who experience purchase problems can get easy access to a dispute resolution process on the same site where they made the purchase. They are not stuck searching for contract terms they likely never read and even more likely lost or failed to retain. This allows all consumers, regardless of power and resources, to feel comfortable seeking assistance.

Online resolution systems also create transparency around seller behavior and raise visibility with outside auditors who may then police market fairness. These regulators may give notice regarding purchase problems, thereby empowering consumers to "vote with their feet" by walking away from underperforming merchants. This transparency is important for addressing the current cynicism in the marketplace. Indeed, shedding light on purchase problems and facilitating resolution of these problems will finally address the structural limitations that have hampered traditional regulatory and legal approaches to online consumer protection.

We do not need to envision these systems from scratch. There have already been several global ODR systems that have tested a variety of approaches and found which work best. A prime example is eBay's ODR system. As the first truly global online e-commerce marketplace, eBay realized it had to provide fast and fair resolutions to all its users, and in response created the largest ODR system in the world to address the challenges consumers face when transacting online. This system has now handled hundreds of millions of disputes, serving as a powerful laboratory for online dispute resolution system design.

It is essential to lay the groundwork for an Internet-wide ODR system that can streamline global e-commerce, generating win-win outcomes for companies and consumers. This new system should incorporate reputation management, transparency, and cutting-edge resolution software to level the playing field and restore consumer confidence. It will be a major step forward in building a new justice system—one that is custom built for the Internet and able to provide fast and fair resolutions to any consumer, no matter in which legal jurisdiction he or she currently resides.

This is not to say that all ODR systems are inherently fair or that shifting from regulatory and judicial resolution to ODR systems will be easy. There are many continuing challenges to keep in mind as these systems are rolled out: ensuring effective enforcement, supporting consolidated and mass resolutions, addressing predispute binding consumer systems, and preserving judicial fora for certain policy-related claims. However, if we can find answers to these questions, then ODR may move us toward a future where universal access to fast and fair redress for online consumers is finally possible. This is vital to fill a void in consumer protection.

The Goal of This Book

The New Handshake is designed to help ODR systems designers, online merchants, payment providers, marketplaces (both tangible goods and services), customer experience designers, lawyers, judges, students, consumer advocates, and policymakers envision and build the next generation of consumer protection. The aim of the book is to provide a context and blueprint for a next-generation consumer-focused redress process that will benefit both consumers and merchants, as well as to help update consumer protection programs to meet the needs and expectations of modern consumers.

The Plan of This Book

This book describes the challenges facing consumers in e-commerce, discusses current strategies for addressing those challenges, details new approaches coming out of e-commerce and ODR, and then offers a design for a consumer-focused global online redress system to achieve those ends. The book then applies this design to several case studies and concludes with a recommended agenda for action.

Part 1 focuses on where we are now. It examines the lack of consumer remedies and customer care in B2C e-commerce. It considers why consumers rarely pursue remedies on purchase complaints and explains how this dynamic undermines economic efficiency and consumer trust. It also details how these market dynamics foster contractual discrimination and enable companies to avoid consumer protection regulations. It then examines what consumers really want from their online redress processes. Finally, it analyzes the lessons learned from eBay's efforts to bolster consumer trust through the creation of a comprehensive system for resolving disputes between buyers and sellers.

Part 2 then looks at the need for resolutions from both the merchant and consumer advocacy perspectives. It lays out the business case for merchant investments in resolution processes, calculating the value of investments in resolutions, focusing especially on reducing costs and increasing future transaction volume. It then discusses how resolution data transparency can benefit consumer protection authorities, consumer advocacy organizations, and policymakers. Finally, it outlines ethical standards that must undergird any process that hopes to be efficient and effective over the long term.

Part 3 distills these observations into a specific set of design criteria. It examines the power imbalances an effective systems design must address to be truly fast and fair. It then details a specific proposed design for a global e-commerce ODR that addresses the challenges facing consumers and merchants in B2C transactions. This part then presents a series of next steps toward making this proposed system a reality and risk factors that could cause the design to fail to achieve its objectives. It then applies the proposed design to a variety of case studies to illustrate how it will work in practice. In conclusion, the book examines what tools and technologies may emerge in the future to make the system more accessible and effective over time.

PART 1

Looking Through the Eyes of Consumers

CHAPTER

1 Where We Are Now

The Internet has empowered consumers in new and exciting ways. It has opened more efficient avenues to buy just about anything. Want proof? Simply pull out your smartphone, swipe your finger across the screen a few times, and presto—your collector's edition Notorious RBG (Ruth Bader Ginsburg) bobblehead is on its way from China. Unfortunately, however, the Internet has not yet delivered on its promise to fundamentally improve consumer protection.

At the dawn of the Internet age, many futurists predicted that technology would shift the balance of power between consumers and merchants in favor of consumers. In his seminal book *The Cluetrain Manifesto* (written in 1999 with Rick Levine, David Weinberger, and Christopher Locke), Doc Searls predicted that technology would usher in a golden age of consumer choice, where buyers would use the wide range of options provided to them by frictionless e-commerce to play merchants off each other, ensuring that consumers got the best deals and the widest selection in every online exchange.

That vision is still a work in progress. In some ways, the Internet has achieved the opposite, ushering in a new age of consumer confusion and disempowerment. Consumers have access to more information than in the past, but many buyers still have a hard time determining which merchants are the most trustworthy. It is also still too hard for consumers to learn how to resolve transaction problems when they arise. Some unscrupulous merchants and marketplaces have leveraged the wide-open, wild-west nature of the Internet to sow even more fear, uncertainty, and doubt among consumers, further preventing them from holding bad merchants accountable. A new breed of fraudster has emerged as well, savvy in the ways of the Internet and skilled at covering their online tracks. In retrospect, the new reach and choice provided by the Internet have unquestionably expanded purchasing options for consumers, but utopian predictions about a golden age of consumer empowerment remain unrealized.

Almost every industry has been reinvented by the expansion of information and communications technology, from medicine to finance to entertainment. However, the redress processes made available to most consumers have not evolved in a similar way. Most resolution options available to consumers resemble those available decades ago: a toll-free number, a complaint form, or an unsatisfying online chat process. For most consumers in the modern era, none of those options sound very appealing. At the same time, small claims court is often unavailable or unsatisfactory for many claims due to jurisdictional limits, long time frames, and other complexities.

Making It Tough for Consumers to Get Solutions

When you last tried to call customer service regarding a complaint, how long were you on hold? Hold times are getting longer—sometimes even as long as an hour. Indeed, reaching a live representative is becoming increasingly difficult. It is therefore no surprise that consumers lament the lack of meaningful access to customer assistance with respect to their purchases.

In an effort to reduce contacts into their customer support centers, some companies are quietly restricting remedies for their consumers. Studies have shown that most consumers are unlikely to read their contracts, let alone understand what the contracts really say. In fact, most consumers ignore contract terms when signing up for a site or service, even when the website requires concrete action, such as clicking a link on a website or scrolling through the terms all the way to the end. Contract terms in e-contracts may go right over the heads of most consumers. They are filled with legalese and are often hidden on obscure web pages. It would take enormous patience and intelligence for the average consumer to read and understand the terms in many common contracts.

At the same time, consumers often assume that they will not really be required to abide by the terms of their contracts. For example, they may figure that companies will be honorable and provide remedies if anything goes wrong. They ignore "fine print" exclusions in the terms and conditions. Consumers also may suffer from overoptimism, cognitive dissonance, and confirmation bias with respect to their purchases. At the time of purchase, most consumers optimistically presume there will not be a problem, so they do not worry about checking out terms or eventual remedies when they click the "accept" box to complete a purchase. Likewise, they want to believe that they have made wise purchasing decisions; thus, when problems do arise, consumers often ignore them in hopes of confirming their wisdom.

As consumers, we also suffer from inertia. We avoid action when signing up for new websites, which prevents us from proactively reading or seeking to change contract terms before we agree. That inertia also hinders consumers from pursuing a claim if it would require them to hire an attorney or to file a claim in court or with an arbitration association. The speed of the Internet and the immediacy of searching, ordering, and receiving items makes us pretty lazy when it comes to reading legal language. Furthermore, pursuing the face-to-face resolution procedures specified in many online terms and conditions requires sophistication and resources that many consumers do not possess. Most consumers do not have the time, money, or education to pursue formal arbitrations or file cases in small claims courts. Indeed, most consumers do not know what arbitration is, much less realize that their contract requires arbitration for any claims that arise.

Merchants also know that consumers very rarely take complaints to the consumer protection agencies, federal regulators, or third parties such as a local chamber of commerce or the Better Business Bureau (BBB). Anger may fuel a consumer's initial e-mail or phone call regarding a purchase problem, but consumers generally do not follow up after receiving no reply or when facing long hold times with customer service. Customer service representatives may also lack authority to provide remedies or make it very stressful for consumers to obtain any redress. All merchants have to do is provide a little procedural complexity and the vast majority of consumers drop the issue.

The Squeaky Wheel System

In the current system, only consumers who are sufficiently motivated to make a lot of noise or pursue options that other consumers would dismiss as too time consuming and frustrating get redress. This creates the squeaky wheel system (SWS) in business-to-consumer (B2C) exchanges. This SWS concept encompasses the notion that the "squeaky wheels" (consumers who are proactive in pursuing their needs and complaints) are most likely to get the assistance, remedies, and other benefits they seek. Meanwhile, those who remain silent because they lack the knowledge, experience, or resources to artfully and actively pursue their interests usually do not receive the same benefits.

Merchants appease the squeaky wheels in order to prevent negative publicity and avoid giving remedies to the majority. They also may point to the resolutions provided to this small number of squeaky wheels as evidence that problems are being resolved. Resolutions are rationed to the customers who make the most noise, while consumers with the least time and resources to learn about, understand, or pursue their claims are left without remedies. Some merchants use the SWS to waylay lawsuits and other public complaints, as well as to keep the majority of consumers unaware of their potential rights. This enables these unscrupulous merchants to save remedy costs and keep claims out of the public eye.

Defenders of the theory that the current market structure promotes efficiency and fairness rely on the power of an informed minority. They argue that, regardless of whether most consumers bargain for efficient contract terms or improved company practices, this informed minority of squeaky wheels will speak for the uninformed masses. The loud voices will pressure companies to improve their contracts and practices or face the risk of lawsuits and negative publicity. However, in-depth studies of this squeaky wheel phenomenon cast doubt on the effectiveness of this informed minority to make meaningful change—let alone the will of a small, vocal group of consumers to advocate for anyone other than themselves.

Complaint systems that suffer from this squeaky wheel syndrome therefore become skewed in favor of the most experienced, educated, and powerful consumers who know how to artfully submit complaints and get what they want. These consumers then have little to no incentive to alert the majority about available remedies, and they become almost complicit in the exploitation of the uninformed majority by reaping the benefits of remedy rationing. At the same time, the interests of this informed minority may not overlap with the interests, needs, or types of claims experienced by the majority.

Merchants may be tempted to manipulate the market by appeasing, and thus quieting, the few sophisticated squeaky wheels who pursue contract changes and remedies when problems arise. Consumers with higher incomes and more education thus end up on top in a consumer caste system. The squeaky wheels expect more and get more from their purchases than those in lower socioeconomic status groups. One study indicated "for every 1,000 purchases, households in the highest status category voice complaints concerning 98.9 purchases, while households in the lowest status category voice complaints concerning 60.7 purchases."

Social Pressures Not to Pursue Redress

Societal influences and stereotypes also play into the SWS and hinder consumers from asserting complaints or getting remedies in person. For example, our society often teaches individuals not to "rock the boat" or complain too much. This is often true for many women, who may be reluctant to assert complaints or pursue their needs due to fear of appearing pushy. Some women also may be less likely than men to recognize opportunities to negotiate. Generally, women also use less assertive language than men when they do pursue negotiations. Similarly, some data has indicated that African American consumers may be less likely than white consumers to realize opportunities to complain regarding their purchases.

Consumers do not get the same deals. Conscious or subconscious biases may lead customer service representatives to offer less advantageous redress options to racial minorities. Studies have shown that African American consumers often do not receive the same purchase benefits as white consumers, regardless of education or income. Data also suggests that consumers in lower socioeconomic status groups often become accustomed to poor treatment. They also may have lower expectations regarding the quality of their purchases and their ability to obtain remedies if problems arise.

Additionally, consumers with a lower socioeconomic status are likely to have fewer resources, lower levels of education, and are more likely to be hindered in asserting themselves due to limited English proficiency. Of course, "status" is an ill-defined term, and no set of assumptions applies universally across all consumer groups.

Nonetheless, data suggest a growing divide between the high-power "haves" and low-power "have-nots" based on income, education, and age.

Furthermore, stereotypes and biases may augment this disparity when individuals interact face-to-face and consciously or subconsciously make assumptions about the other based on race, gender, and age. This goes both ways. On the one hand, conscious and subconscious biases of customer service associates may affect how they treat consumers and lead them to offer less advantageous deals to racial and ethnic minorities and women. On the other hand, consumers also may make assumptions about customer service associates, which may impact their interactions and impede their access to remedies. Furthermore, consumers may perpetuate their own low-power status by assuming that they will be unfairly judged or brushed aside. These forces combine to undermine equal protection for all consumers.

A Broken System for Consumer Redress

The SWS, along with its related behavioral and sociological propensities, hinders the ability of consumers to get fast and fair resolutions. It also focuses attention on a small set of data points instead of examining consumer redress holistically across all transactions, which keeps consumer issues off the radar of courts and government regulators. It also hinders consumers' access to information that would assist them in "voting with their feet" by choosing to avoid or leave companies that have bad track records with respect to the goods and services they provide. The SWS advantages consumers who already enjoy disproportionate power due to social or economic status and provides that vocal minority with disproportionate benefits.

Of course, there are legitimate arguments against these critiques. For example, some law and economics theorists posit that strict contract enforcement results in an optimal allocation of resources overall, even if a few consumers lose out on their claims. They suggest that consumers transact with businesses who are constantly competing with each other, and that this competition forces companies to continuously strive to keep their consumers happy. As a result, merchants will provide redress and solve consumer problems to secure market advantages over their competitors.

In reality, however, most consumers do not have perfect information about the market and do not read or understand their rights, let alone the complicated terms commonly appearing in form contracts. Consumers therefore fail to purchase optimal quantities or bargain for competitive and efficient terms. Moreover, they often fail to realize their rights or the remedies that they deserve. This lack of clarity undercuts the efficient free market dynamics that might otherwise urge businesses to make problem resolution a priority. This enables bad actors to take advantage of consumers' lack of information and bargaining power. It is therefore unlikely that consumers are informed and market forces are adequate to ensure the ongoing fairness or efficiency of consumer redress processes.

For example, researchers who studied consumers' Internet browsing behavior on 66 online software companies' websites found that only one or two out of one thousand shoppers actually accessed the companies' standard form contracts (referred to as end-user software license agreements, or EULAs). Furthermore, they found that shoppers rarely read product reviews or otherwise seek information about the terms and conditions of their purchases. Think about your own behavior: When was the last time you actually read through a user agreement before clicking the "I accept" option?

Similarly, it is unlikely that a sufficient number of proactive consumers will regulate merchant practices by spreading information and taking action regarding purchase problems. One European study found that only 7 percent of consumer cases ended with a resolution that was made public. The researchers also found that 45 percent of launched complaints ended with no agreement or decision, suggesting that consumers who took initial action on their complaints gave up their pursuit along the way. While some complaints may truly lack merit, the study's findings suggest that perhaps even initially proactive consumers are unlikely to continue a fight to the benefit of themselves, let alone all consumers.

Furthermore, it is becoming more difficult for consumers to be informed about their rights and remedies due to the high costs of obtaining information and pursing contract claims. For example, of the nearly two-thirds of *Consumer Reports* survey respondents who claimed that they actually read all of the disclosures regarding a new loan or credit card, only 16 percent found the disclosures easy to understand. Additionally, well-meaning policymakers have advanced disclosure laws aimed to address information asymmetries that often leave consumers in the dark about their rights. However, these seemingly pro-consumer rules often backfire by adding to the information overload that already clouds consumers' comprehension of their agreements. Adding more legal clauses, even if they are in all caps or printed in red type, does not solve consumer confusion—it just adds to the problem.

The advent of big data has added to this challenge. Data brokers gather vast amounts of information about consumers, and some businesses now use it to determine how each buyer will be treated in the marketplace. Such data collection is often benign when consumers initially give their consent, and it is presented to the user initially as being beneficial for them because it will help to tailor experiences to the specific needs and interests of each individual consumer. However, the data collected can also be used to disadvantage buyers. Collected data may lead to differential pricing or exemptions from cash-back or layaway purchase options, effectively redlining some consumers without their knowledge or consent. In this way, big data can increase information asymmetry between merchants and consumers.

Most consumers feel powerless when seeking remedies regarding their purchases. They just presume they have no say in how they are treated or what resolution options will be made available to them. For example, studies have shown that the majority of cellular phone customers feel they must submit to price increases and added charges, and that it is fruitless to protest. This is especially true when the consumer does not have time or resources to research available options and is striving to retain cellular services in a market dominated by relatively few companies due to consolidation. Consumers are acutely aware that oligarchic market conditions, such as those in the telecommunications industry, give companies great power to set the terms. Consumers feel the game is rigged against them, without any way to change the system.

Class Actions

The most common kind of consumer mass claim in the United States is the class action. When a group of consumers all experience the same problem in interacting with a business, those buyers are eligible to join a *class*, which is represented by lead plaintiffs and one lawyer or group of lawyers. Once the class is certified by a judge, the lawyer representing the class can approach the business, explain the nature of the class action, and outline an appropriate remedy. The individual claimants generally have no initial costs. Instead, the lawyers who convene the class cover the costs to pursue the case, but later take a prescribed percentage of the eventual settlement or award. This can benefit consumers when they do not have to attend hearings, pay any costs, or invest any time or money in the proceedings. However, these processes can go on for years, and they often do not result in perfect or complete redress.

At the same time, businesses often face a difficult choice when presented with a class action. They can bear the costs and negative publicity of fighting the class action in court, or they can quickly settle to end the action. Businesses fear class actions because they usually take years to defend and cost businesses a great deal in legal fees with no guarantee of a beneficial outcome. Some of the class actions that have gone to trial have generated surprisingly costly decisions against the businesses in question. Moreover, the negative publicity alone can close a vulnerable business. Accordingly, businesses usually settle class actions based on simple cost calculations. The legal costs may be projected to exceed the value of the payout or the bad press generated by the class action may be too onerous for the business to bear.

Class actions are intended to hold businesses accountable for their behavior. They may punish bad actors and create financial incentives for businesses to do the right thing by their customers or face financial consequences. For very serious issues (e.g., drugs that caused serious injuries or death, communities that suffered from pollution of the water supply caused by secretly dumping chemicals), class actions may be the best way to get justice. Big payouts may go a long way toward providing justice to individuals and families victimized in these ways, and businesses may be more careful in their future dealings if they know the risk of a class action exists.

For an online consumer, however, the experience of participating in a class action is decidedly mixed. On the one hand, online consumers may end up in a class action without being aware that there was ever a problem in the first place.

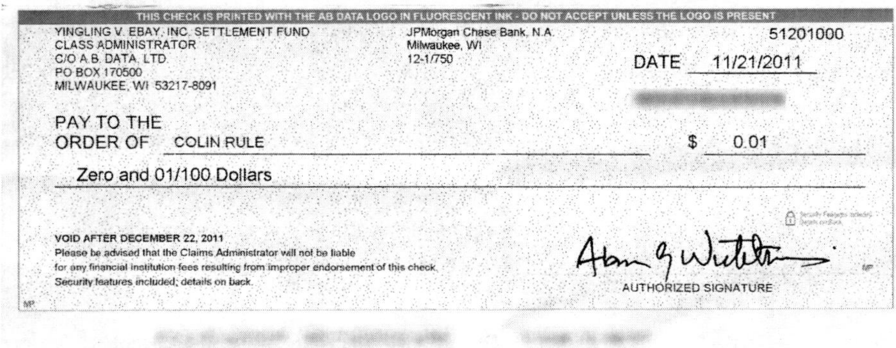

THIS CHECK IS PRINTED WITH THE AB DATA LOGO IN FLUORESCENT INK - DO NOT ACCEPT UNLESS THE LOGO IS PRESENT

YINGLING V. EBAY, INC. SETTLEMENT FUND
CLASS ADMINISTRATOR
C/O A.B. DATA, LTD.
PO BOX 170500
MILWAUKEE, WI 53217-8091

JPMorgan Chase Bank, N.A.
Milwaukee, WI
12-1/750

51201000

DATE 11/21/2011

PAY TO THE ORDER OF COLIN RULE $ 0.01

Zero and 01/100 Dollars

VOID AFTER DECEMBER 22, 2011
Please be advised that the Claims Administrator will not be liable for any financial institution fees resulting from improper endorsement of this check.
Security features included; details on back.

AUTHORIZED SIGNATURE

Figure 1.1 The one-cent class action settlement check.

Consider the consumer who was perfectly happy with a purchase, but nonetheless gets the free coupon or check in the mail as part of a class of harmed consumers. A consumer has the freedom to opt out of a class action, but most are happy to join when it is as easy as filling out some paperwork, waiting for the process to play out, and getting a check in the mail.

Nonetheless, there are many consumers who are harmed twice: first through the purchase (deception, defects, etc.) and second when seeking to actually get a remedy through a class action process. This is because in the usual online consumer scenario, the class action process takes years. Consumers frequently receive relatively paltry payouts, while lawyers may reap much higher profits due to the large number of consumers affected. Many of us have the experience of being opted into a class and waiting several years to get a tiny reimbursement. As you can see in Figure 1.1, Colin received a one-cent reimbursement check from a class action that was filed against eBay (Colin's former employer). The issue targeted by the class action was a seemingly trivial matter—a slightly higher charge for items within a certain category of the eBay marketplace. Colin did not opt into this class; he was opted in by the lawyers who filed the case and who did not require Colin to fill out any paperwork. The class action administrators paid 44 cents for a stamp to mail Colin this one-cent check.

Why would anyone bother to file a class action for a one-cent reimbursement? They wouldn't. However, the lawyers who filed the case ended up making tens of millions of dollars when eBay decided to settle. There were many millions of eBay customers in the class that was pulled together by these lawyers. Although each individual eBay user did not make much money, the percentage awarded to the law firms who pushed the class action was quite substantial.

Amy had a similar experience when she was opted into a class action against a cell phone provider but received no real payout. Instead, she merely received a coupon that would have required her to continue buying from that provider. Meanwhile, the lawyers gathered legal fees and announced victory. There are even some class actions where the consumers get nothing but the lawyers still get their payout. For example, in a recent privacy class action settled with Yahoo, the consumers in the class who had their privacy violated got no reimbursement, but the lawyers who filed the case made millions of dollars. Many readers of this book likely have similar stories.

As in any type of court case, there are both justified class actions and unjustified class actions. There are definitely examples of abuse, but there are also many examples of justice being done. The question is this: Do class action lawsuits provide a resolution experience that best protects online consumers? We would argue that the answer to the question is no. Buyers want fast and fair resolutions—preferably in minutes or days, not weeks or months or years. A good chunk of the benefits in these e-commerce class actions go to the lawyers, not the consumers who are ostensibly the wronged parties. There are so many costs and procedural requirements in the class action system that the lawyers usually end up getting paid a good bit of the money that should be going to the consumers directly. The class action process is too slow and too inefficient to provide the kind of redress that online consumers say they want.

The Growth of Binding Arbitration Clauses for Consumers

Consumer class actions have been severely constrained by regulatory changes in consumer arbitration over the past few years. Over that time, the Supreme Court has become increasingly pro-business in enforcing predispute arbitration clauses in B2C contracts. This really came to a head in 2013 with the Supreme Court's decision in *AT&T v. Concepcion*. That case significantly increased the power of a business to block class actions by enabling businesses to include a predispute arbitration clause with a class action waiver in their consumer contracts. State courts had been using state contract defenses to limit enforcement of these clauses, but the Court in *AT&T* held that the Federal Arbitration Act preempted state courts (specifically, the California court) from applying a general contract defense to preclude enforcement of the arbitration clause in AT&T's consumer contract.

After that decision, there was an immediate wave of General Counsels integrating *Concepcion*-style arbitration clauses into their companies' terms and conditions. If you check the terms for your bank account, credit card, cell phone, or favorite website, you are likely to find this type of waiver. Many companies were relieved to finally have a way to protect themselves from class action exposure through the use of these clauses. The clauses often direct consumers to submit their claims in face-to-face arbitration procedures that require an immediate deposit of filing and administrative fees. This deposit hinders consumers' incentive to file a claim, especially when the initial filing and administration costs outweigh any potential recovery through the procedure. This is true even if consumers may be able to recoup fees when an award is made in their favor.

Perhaps most importantly, these clauses nearly always preclude class proceedings of any kind. It does not take much analysis to conclude that the primary focus of these clauses is to block consumers from joining any kind of class or combined proceeding. Indeed, common arbitration clauses even specify that they become inoperative if a court or arbitrator finds the class action waiver component of the clause unenforceable for any reason. Many companies would rather litigate than face class or consolidated arbitration proceedings.

This class action issue in arbitration has caught the eye of the Consumer Financial Protection Bureau (CFPB), the federal consumer advocacy organization championed by Elizabeth Warren and now run by Richard Cordray. The CFPB was given authority by the Dodd-Frank Act to investigate the use of these predispute consumer arbitration clauses and issue regulations with respect to consumer financial products and services. After an in-depth investigation of consumer arbitration, the CFPB identified these class waivers as problematic. A draft regulation was proposed to ban the use of these predispute arbitration clauses if they preclude consumers from joining a class action.

Based on the statistics shared by the CFPB and case filing data, arbitration clauses that bar class actions usually halt consumers' access to remedies for small-dollar claims. Most consumers simply are not using face-to-face arbitration options to get redress. Hundreds of thousands (even millions) of consumers obtain some level of redress, however small, from class actions each year. In contrast, very few consumers exercise their right to arbitration each year. That volume differential provides a stark reason to be concerned about how these arbitration clauses and class action waivers work in tandem to stymie consumer redress.

Again, it generally makes no economic sense for a consumer to pay hundreds or thousands of dollars in filing fees and travel costs to assert an individual claim regarding a modest amount of money. Take the example of a defective cellular phone that costs $300. It may be worthwhile for a consumer to join a class action with many other consumers who have faced similar problems with their phones, even if the consumer only gets $150 in the final settlement after paying the attorneys. However, the same consumer would not have that option if there is a predispute arbitration clause in their contract. Consumers would have to act on their own, and pay arbitration filing and administrative fees, in the hopes of recouping the fees in an eventual award. Most consumers quickly conclude that it is simply not worthwhile to pursue redress through arbitration, especially when taking into account the time and hassle of a face-to-face proceeding.

The new CFPB regulations will not help that cellular phone customer. Cellular phone contracts are not financial products or services, and the CFPB only has the authority to regulate financial institutions. Additionally, as of the time of writing this book, the CFPB had not issued final regulations regarding its proposal to prohibit companies from including predispute arbitration clauses in agreements regarding financial products or services that prevent class action lawsuits. Indeed, it remains unclear whether anything will change regarding the enforcement of arbitration clauses.

Mandatory arbitration provisions also privatize dispute resolution, which enable companies to potentially design their own arbitration processes. These processes are often quite different from the consumer redress options available in the courts. For example, most private arbitration processes keep private the outcomes achieved by consumers. This may limit public access to information regarding faulty products and company improprieties. Without public knowledge of these filings and their outcomes, it can be difficult to uncover products that should be recalled and inform other affected consumers about their eligibility for redress. For example, a 2010 *Consumer Reports* survey found that less than a quarter of the respondents said they researched product recalls; only a fifth of the respondents were aware of recalls regarding products they had purchased in the past three years. Furthermore, "an additional 15 percent simply threw the product in the trash rather than returning it for a refund, an exchange, or a free repair." Keeping resolutions confidential stymies regulation of defective products, which may place consumers at increased risk of harm. Furthermore, it again suggests a need for expanded and readily accessible systems that lower the hurdles to obtaining remedies and raise expectations regarding customer care.

Limitations on Legal Redress Options for Online Consumers

Even if consumers retain their rights to pursue legal recourse for a transaction problem, the legal system can be difficult to utilize. Face-to-face processes of any kind are often infeasible for many consumers. Individuals lack the time, money, knowledge, and patience to pursue even small claims court proceedings. People busy with work and family obligations are likely to give up pursuing complaints when companies ignore their initial requests for assistance.

In addition, the courts are still very much tied to geography and jurisdiction. To decide how to resolve a legal case, it first must be established which law applies. The same case can potentially have very different outcomes based on which law governs the resolution process. These days, however, which law applies is no longer a simple question to answer. A buyer in Brazil may purchase an item from a seller in France from a marketplace based in the United States, and the item may be shipped directly to the buyer from a warehouse in China. Which law applies should a problem arise? If the item is only worth $100, what lawyer would be willing to take the case to hammer out the complex jurisdictional questions? Which judge would have the power or aptitude to hear that case?

Even if a consumer decides to file a case in court, why should the merchant care if the merchant is not subject to the jurisdiction of the court where the case is filed? If a consumer in Colorado buys an item from a merchant in Berlin and experiences a problem, why would the German merchant care if the consumer filed a complaint in a small claims court in Denver? How is it reasonable to ask the consumer to retain counsel in Germany to file a case in the merchant's home jurisdiction, if the value of the purchase is only a couple hundred dollars and the cost of retaining a lawyer is several times that?

Consumer protection authorities face similar challenges. If a citizen reports a problem with a domestic seller, their local or national consumer protection agency has the authority to investigate the matter and potentially take enforcement action against the merchant. If a citizen reports a problem with an international seller, the consumer protection agency has no legal authority to pursue the matter. As citizens increasingly engage in cross-border and international transactions powered by the reach of new communication technologies, national and regional consumer protection authorities are continuing to lose ground in helping to protect their citizens. Very few systems are in place to enable regional and national consumer protection agencies and advocates to help consumers who have been victimized by merchants outside of their home geography. This challenge will only get bigger as e-commerce continues to expand.

Crossing the Digital Divide

In the early 2000s, the biggest obstacle to expanding access to justice through technology was called the "digital divide." The concern was that only wealthy people could afford technology and fast Internet connections, so technology-powered systems would disproportionally benefit the affluent. Many public investments in technology were put off due to this concern. Since then, however, the dynamics have changed significantly. The introduction of inexpensive mobile phones has democratized access to the Internet. There has been an increase in the number of individuals and households who have Internet access, but concerns about the digital divide persist based primarily on educational attainment, age, and household income. For example, the Pew Research Center (PRC) found in its 2013 study of broadband use that approximately 70 percent of adults had a high-speed broadband connection to the Internet, while 3 percent had a home dial-up connection. Home broadband use was greatest for white, non-Hispanic (74 percent) and lowest for Hispanic (53 percent) consumers.

The PRC also found that smartphone usage has created new means for accessing the Internet, especially for minority groups and those with lower economic means. For example, 10 percent of Americans do not have home broadband Internet access, but most of these consumers do own a smartphone. Smartphones also virtually eliminate the digital divide among races and ethnicities, with 80 percent of white non-Hispanic, 79 percent of black non-Hispanic, and 75 percent of Hispanic individuals having some Internet access through home broadband or a smartphone. Still, smartphones widen the digital divide between 18- to 29-year-olds and those who are over age 65 (increasing from a gap of 37 percentage points in home broadband access to a gap of 49 percentage points when taking smartphones into account).

In the past, landline telephones were also considered to be luxuries, available only to the affluent. Over time, however, telephone access expanded to the point where public bodies were comfortable providing services via the telephone. It appears that Internet access is at a similar tipping point. Policymakers and agencies now see the value of utilizing technology to deliver services more efficiently and effectively, and many now believe technology will help them get access to underprivileged populations. A phone manufacturer in India recently announced it was selling a smartphone for $7, and the government has begun giving out free tablets to school children. It appears that the price of these technologies has fallen to a point where it is reasonable to presume near ubiquity in terms of Internet access, presuming all services are also optimized to be delivered through a mobile device in addition to a desktop experience.

Credit Card Chargebacks

Some consumer advocates have argued that the best model currently available for protecting consumers is the credit card chargeback process. Under that process, consumers can contact their credit card issuer to reverse charges in transactions where the consumer was dissatisfied, even if the merchant disagrees. The chargeback system was originally put in place at the request of public consumer advocates and Attorneys General, and it does go a long way toward empowering consumers and creating a more level playing field.

However, the chargeback process is not essentially a resolution process. The chargeback system does not enable a conversation between the buyer and the seller to work out a transaction problem. The buyer participates in the process through their card issuer and the seller through their merchant services provider, making collaboration extremely difficult. If the buyer files a chargeback, the merchant is charged a fee and the payment is immediately reversed from the merchant's account back to the consumer's account. Merchants must often keep a deposit on file to fund these immediate reversals. If the merchant disagrees with the chargeback, they can "re-present" the charge, and the money is reversed again. Each reversal involves an additional fee. Eventually, if the parties are determined enough, the case can be escalated to an arbitration administered by the card network. However, the cost of that arbitration can be prohibitive, and only a tiny volume of cases reach that level. Many merchants just give up when they receive a chargeback because the chances of successful reversal are so low and the effort to contest it is so great.

As a result, the chargeback system is less of a resolution process and more of a liability shift. The system was not designed to resolve disputes via mutual agreement. Most merchants hate the chargeback system because they feel it gives too much power to the buyers; however, because credit cards are so ubiquitous, merchants have no choice but to accept credit card payments. Also, the credit card networks make money from the fees charged upon every reversal, while they also make money from the high interest rates charged to consumers who do not pay off their full balance every month.

Chargebacks are also not a universal right. In Canada and North America, the chargeback process is very generous, with consumers able to file chargebacks for all kinds of issues, including nonreceipt and item quality disputes. In other regions, chargebacks are only allowed in cases of fraud or identity theft. Consumers are often unaware of their credit card chargeback rights, which means filing volumes are very low. Because of the costs associated with credit card payments, many merchants are trying to shift their payments onto debit or automated clearing house (ACH) networks, which have no chargeback rights other than fraud and unauthorized payment reversals. Some geographies rely heavily on bank transfers or stored value wallets, which also have inconsistent reversal rights. Therefore, although we can learn quite a bit from the chargeback system, it is not a viable solution for expanding consumer redress around the world.

Envisioning a New Process

All of these challenges in trying to provide effective redress to consumers have created momentum behind an effort to change the way we think about consumer protection. The old zero-sum debate between consumer advocates (presumed to be in collaboration with the class action bar) and the big legal defense firms (presumed to be doing the bidding of big corporations) has achieved little in terms of progress over the past few decades. Each side has continued to point fingers, with businesses supposedly abusing customers and class action attorneys supposedly filing frivolous cases to force settlement. The debate over predispute binding arbitration clauses is only the latest phase in this ongoing back and forth.

However, the Internet has continued to change the game, even while this zero-sum debate was playing out in the courts and legislatures. In fact, while few were paying attention, some of the promising dynamics that had been identified by the Internet futurists, such as Doc Searls in the 1990s, have begun to pan out. Consumers are getting more skilled at using the Internet to organize, and the wide spectrum of choice is moving toward more trustworthy merchants and marketplaces. Although the regulators and lawyers were debating minimum standards and binding arbitration clauses, leading e-commerce businesses were going far beyond legal requirements for consumer protection. Forward-thinking merchants are creating next-generation systems that can handle consumer problems. Entirely new types of companies, sometimes called "sharing economy" or "collaborative" companies, are being started by consumers for other consumers. They are bringing a whole new attitude to consumer protection.

Large Internet intermediaries, such as online marketplaces (eBay), large merchants (Amazon), and payment processors (Paypal), realized very early on that the consumer trust problem was creating friction on the Internet; by solving it, they could provide a valuable market advantage. These companies were not willing to wait for regulators to figure out how to provide online consumer protection, so they moved to build their own solutions to address the problem. For these large Internet companies, trust in transactions proved to be a powerful competitive differentiator—one with a demonstrably positive impact on the bottom line.

Many forward-thinking consumer protection organizations began to recognize this trend as well. They saw that these new Internet platforms were creating next-generation redress systems that were delivering fast and fair resolutions to consumers, all within the private sector. Instead of falling back into the old finger pointing between business and consumer advocates, a new zone of cooperation emerged to offer some reason for optimism. The 2003 agreement between Consumers International and the Global Business Dialogue on eCommerce (GBDe) was an important step in this direction. Suddenly, two groups that had long been tugging on either end of the rope and getting nowhere were finding ways to join the same side, working together with a common purpose.

Regulators also came to the conclusion that court-based approaches to consumer protection were destined to fail in an Internet-powered economy. Longstanding efforts to resolve jurisdictional questions around consumer disputes, such as The Hague Conference on Private International Law, were not getting any closer to agreement despite decades of negotiation. A proposition to legally locate all consumer disputes in the home jurisdiction of the consumer was presented by the Canadian and Brazilian delegations to the Organization of American States (OAS) in 2009, but the concept was met with quite a bit of resistance. How could Internet merchants defend themselves in every jurisdiction around the world? The concept seemed out of step with where the economy was going.

In response to the Brazilian and Canadian proposal, the U.S. State Department offered a blueprint for the use of online dispute resolution (ODR) to build a global, cross-border system for resolving consumer disputes. The proposal was met with such enthusiasm that UNCITRAL (the United Nations agency responsible for harmonizing global laws) decided to devote a working group to the concept. The European Standards organization, the International Standards Organization, and the Canadian legislature all quietly issued standards for quality ODR. It was clear a consensus was building.

In fact, the Organisation for Economic Co-operation and Development (OECD) Committee on Consumer Policy recently released a draft recommendation from the Council of Consumer Protection in eCommerce that reads, in part:

> *Consumers should have access to [alternative dispute resolution] ADR mechanisms, including online dispute resolution systems, to facilitate the resolution of claims over e-commerce transactions, with special attention to low value or cross-border transactions. Although such mechanisms may be financially supported in a variety of ways, they should be designed to provide dispute resolution on an objective, impartial, and consistent basis, with individual outcomes independent of influence by those providing financial or other support.*

The OECD document also states that "the development by businesses of internal complaints handling mechanisms, which enable consumers to informally resolve their complaints directly with businesses, at the earliest possible stage, without charge, should be encouraged." For an organization focused on consumer protection to be specifically calling on merchants to build their own private resolution processes is a big breakthrough, as well as an indicator of how universal these sentiments have become.

The Civil Justice Council in the United Kingdom conducted an extended study of ODR in civil cases, eventually recommending that the Ministry of Justice create something called "Her Majesty's Online Court," which could resolve all cases under £25,000 through ODR mechanisms. As Lord Justice Fulford, the Senior Presiding Judge of England and Wales, put it, "ODR will be an integral part of the going [court] digitalization process. It is absolutely necessary for the survival of the justice system in the UK." Similar conclusions are being reached by judicial luminaries around the world. After much study and inquiry, they are concluding that we cannot update our old legal redress systems to keep up with the digital age. The old way of providing justice is broken, and we need to build for the future. Software-enabled resolution processes are seen by many thought leaders as a much better fit with the needs of online consumers than legal redress options.

A Window of Opportunity

We are now at an inflection point in the worldwide adoption of ODR. UNCITRAL's ODR Working Group has just released their final report, backed by years of negotiations involving 66 national delegations, which urges governments and judiciaries to expand global availability of ODR for consumers. Brazil has just implemented a law that requires mandatory mediation for all consumer cases in the courts, and specifically recommends ODR as a fast and cost-effective option. British Columbia is launching an online court based on ODR, called the Civil Resolution Tribunal, which will handle civil consumer filings up to $10,000 in value. The UK's Civil Aviation Authority has also launched an ODR process to resolve consumer complaints against airlines.

Perhaps the most stunning example is the new European Union Regulation on Online Dispute Resolution for Consumer Disputes, which took effect in January 2016. This legislative instrument sets up a framework for online dispute resolution to handle national and cross-border issues within the European Union. All merchants established in member states are required to inform European consumers about the availability of ODR on their website and in e-mail communications. The European Union has even constructed a government-hosted ODR filing page to make case filing simple for consumers. Cases filed on the EU page are immediately routed to national ADR service providers located in the appropriate geographies.

The EU ODR regulation is a major step forward, but it only governs consumers and merchants within the European Union. Thus, consumers outside of the European Union do not have an equivalent system should they encounter a problem. In fact, all consumers around the world should be eligible for similar redress processes. That is why these advances, and the emerging consensus behind them, are opening a window of opportunity. Now is the time to build the next generation of consumer protection, powered by ODR.

CHAPTER 2

What Consumers Want

With all of this back and forth about class actions and predispute binding arbitration clauses, we may be losing sight of the most important question of all: What is it that consumers really want? If we are interested in helping consumers, we need to focus our attention specifically on that question. In this chapter, we take a closer look at consumer protection through the eyes of the modern consumer.

Technology Is Changing Consumers' Lives

Consumers from around the world use websites such as Facebook, Google, and Amazon to communicate with friends, manage their daily schedules, and purchase items. It is easy to call up any of these sites on our laptops or smartphones with a single click. We have come to expect that they will be available to us 24 hours a day, 7 days a week. We also expect that the usability of these sites will constantly improve, adding features and functionality on an ongoing basis. We rely on these tools every day, so we need them to be always available and extremely intuitive.

Now, we are bringing the expectations set by these sites into other areas of our lives. We use the Internet to make health insurance elections, rebalance a 401(k), or sign up kids for summer camp. Mark Andreesen has said that "software is eating the world," and it is not hard to see how that is true in nearly every area of our day-to-day lives. Many administrative tasks have moved or are moving onto the Internet, from paying taxes to buying groceries. Now, when a government agency requires an in-person appearance to certify a document or a claims department requires a letter to be faxed, your immediate thought may be, "How inefficient! How 'old school.' This isn't the way the world works anymore. They need to get their act together and move into the 21st century."

It used to be that only big businesses transacted across borders. Now, technology enables individual consumers to cross borders like never before. You can communicate with anyone in the world with just a few swipes of your fingers on a tablet. As a result, our lives more easily cross boundaries. We are all now cross-jurisdictional. Technology is flattening the world, creating connections that span the globe in milliseconds, bouncing along fiber-optic cables at the bottom of the ocean, or beaming data between satellites. We are now more globally connected than at any other time in human history, and the pace of that connection is continuing to accelerate.

The online world also enables a new level of transparency. Any factual question that pops into your head can likely be answered with just a couple of clicks into Google and Wikipedia. We now take for granted that all the information of the world is at our fingertips, from obscure 1980s pop songs to the complete writings of Diderot. We are all publishers now. We can post our musings at any moment, making them instantly accessible to every other Internet user in the world.

Technology also enables collaboration. These online tools and communication environments enable us to interact with each other in ways that were impractical, if not impossible, before. This kind of online cooperation is also becoming the heart of many professions. Employers recruit individuals with skills to collaborate with teams around the country and around the world. In the e-commerce context, when an issue arises, buyers can immediately reach out to their sellers to seek a solution. Updated tracking information is readily available. Online discussion environments make it easy to diagnose problems, share photos and files, and coordinate next steps. The ability to collaborate online with others to jointly resolve problems is increasingly seen as the new normal.

These changes are altering the way consumers expect to resolve their transaction problems. Studies conducted by the government of British Columbia have revealed that despite greater self-reported satisfaction with in-person and phone-based support than with online interactions, individuals still prefer online interactions. When problems arise with a transaction, modern consumers want and expect to be able to use technology to get the problems resolved.

Many consumers are not willing to take time off work to drive down to an office to file a small claims dispute. They are not willing to fill out a paper class-action form, mail it in, and wait two years for a resolution. Instead, consumers want quick and easy resolutions. They expect to be able to effortlessly share information about their purchase experiences and to consult information shared by others. Consumers now rely on this online information to identify bad merchants and avoid buying from them. The types of solutions that have been provided to consumers in the past (e.g., class actions, arbitrations, toll-free numbers) are no longer in line with these new expectations. As a result, consumer remedy systems must adapt or become obsolete. The old systems are being measured against new consumer expectations.

Aunt Prue

Sometimes when designing a new resolution flow, we ask each other what Aunt Prue would think. In software design, you are taught to follow the KISS principle (Keep It Simple, Stupid). One way to do that is to think about how you would explain the process you are designing to your mother. If you cannot summarize it in a way that she would understand in five minutes, you need to simplify your process. However, if your mother is not the right archetype for this exercise (maybe she has a PhD in electrical engineering), you can use Aunt Prue.

Aunt Prue is a friendly grandmother from someplace in the Midwestern United States who has purchased a low-dollar value item online—maybe a Hummel figurine or a needlepoint pattern. (The fact that Prue sounds like a good grandmotherly name is a bonus, because Prue is also an acronym for "problem resolution user experience.") All Prue wants is to make her purchase and get the item, as described, a few days later. But sadly, a problem arises. Maybe a week later the item still has not arrived, or maybe it did arrive and it was not what Prue was expecting. Suddenly, the excitement Prue felt when she bought the item changes to trepidation and irritation that getting the problem fixed will waste her time.

Customer service leaders spend a lot of time thinking about how to delight their customers. Sometimes, companies will spend large sums on outbound calls to customers, loyalty awards, and gift cards, which are all aimed at pushing up satisfaction and delivering "wow" moments. However, the more we looked at the situation through Aunt Prue's eyes, the more we realized that she just wanted her problem solved. She didn't want check-in calls from gregarious customer service representatives, or gift cards, or even fancy e-mails with status updates and trackers. All she wants is to quickly solve the problem and get the item she originally purchased. She essentially wants to revive the "good old days" when one could conclude a purchase with a handshake, and trust that the seller would correct any later problems. Prue wants a *New Handshake*—an online remedy mechanism that replicates the trust and responsibility the physical handshake provided. She doesn't need a bumper sticker, a 5 percent off coupon, or a free latte at Starbucks. She just wants a solution, and she wants it to be easy.

Aunt Prue is not alone. Research indicates that consumers do not think about their purchase problems in legal terms. They do not consult or care about their purchase contracts, and they certainly do not want to deal with lawyers. If my new curling iron breaks after one use, I am not running to a lawyer to file a Magnuson Moss Warranty Act claim. I am tossing it in the trash or e-mailing the seller to get a refund. If the seller asks for any extra steps or makes resolution tough, I am likely to give up and just go buy a new one (while vowing to never buy from that seller again). Getting a coupon in the mail for 25 percent off my next purchase would seem condescending and annoying. I just want a quick, full refund or a new iron that works. That is also the extent of Prue's feelings when she thinks about consumer protection.

Race to the Bottom in Customer Care

The problem is that even Prue's very simple requirements are not being met for most of her online purchases. Many consumers are not getting fast and effective solutions when problems arise. Instead, they feel battered and bruised by poor customer support, and they feel ignored or undervalued. Almost every large business maintains a large call center filled by an army of thousands of customer service representatives (CSRs) in headsets, responding to every incoming customer inquiry on a first-in, first-out basis. Sometimes these centers are located in the United States, but many are now being relocated overseas, largely for cost reasons. Customers dial the toll-free number and a phone tree sorts the incoming calls to different teams, who then assign them to individual customer service representatives to be worked one at a time via voice communication. Waiting on hold, forced to listen to bad music and advertisements, drives consumers crazy. (I bet you can clearly recall the voice in your head saying, "Please listen closely, because our menu options have recently changed.")

Most business executives—even those who value customer satisfaction—view customer support (often called "Operations" or "Ops") as a necessary evil. Every business has to take phone calls, they reason, so the company just needs to bite the bullet and fund the agents. Call centers cost a staggering amount of money because thousands of CSRs have to be paid hourly for the work they do. Call centers are usually considered as purely a cost to be carried on the bottom line—unavoidably necessary, but definitely not a driver of profit to the business in any way.

Customer service representatives have a tough job. It is not easy to handle an endless stream of calls all day, talking with aggrieved people. It takes a toll. The average tenure for a CSR is less than a year, although reps who make it through their time on the front lines can get promoted to management positions, where they often last for much longer. Training a CSR can take two or three months, so with that turnover, it is an extremely expensive proposition to maintain a world-class call center staff. A constant stream of new reps must be coming through the door for training to take the seats of the CSRs who are on their way out.

Contact traffic usually comes into customer support centers in bursts, often because centers are only open for limited hours and many customers call at the same time (for instance, on their lunch breaks). Call centers can get backed up by these surges, which generate long delays for customers waiting for a representative to pick up the phone. In some cases, CSRs may not be empowered to resolve the issue the customer is calling about. They often can do little more than read customers the policy in question and leave the matter there. At the same time, the minority of higher value customers can get escalated to senior CSRs, who have more authority to push matters up the chain. In this way, customer service centers also function as unofficial "squeaky wheel" training centers because loud complaining can definitely get more results. Silent sufferers, who just meekly accept their fate and hang up, tend to get the short end of the stick. Therefore, customers are incentivized to make threats and demands because it sometimes pays off. Consumers have to be persistent and tenacious to get results.

Customer support is a hard job, and it is difficult to find people who really love it. Even the name—"support"—can grate on people (you provide support to someone who is experiencing emotional distress or is in mourning, not someone you are working with to solve a problem). Except for more advanced routing and tracking tools, customer support works pretty much the same way it did in the 1970s, with people answering the phones and trying to remain civil and friendly in the face of continuous complaints and demands. For a customer, having to pick up the phone and call the support number is simultaneously frustrating and aggravating. It means wasted time, with potentially even more frustration and aggravation if the issue cannot be resolved on one call. For the company, having any customer make a call to customer service is a failure. As soon as the call is received, profit is lost—perhaps more profit than was made on the transaction in the first place. In addition, having to pay a CSR to tell your customer that there is nothing that can be done, thus generating frustration and harming loyalty, is a bad deal all around.

Some people will argue that having consumers interact with live customer support agents helps to personalize the relationship between the consumer and the business. This recalls the discussion that took place when banks started installing automated teller machines (ATMs) in the 1980s. Critics suggested the machines would not be used because bank customers would not trust them to handle money. What if you withdrew $100 and the machine gave you $80? Also, the presumption was that customers wanted to know their bankers personally, so they would skip the ATMs. Think about your own life now, 30 years later. When was the last time you went into a bank? ATMs have now become so smart that you can give them a stack of dirty checks and they will scan them all and add up the total for you. Some of them will even sell you stamps. They almost never make a mistake and have even become the norm for getting foreign currency when traveling abroad. No one goes to banks to get currency before traveling any more, and travelers' checks are a thing of the past. The experience with ATMs is a pretty good harbinger of what is coming soon in the world of customer support.

At the same time, companies are cutting down on live customer support to save money, and many seem to be investing less in training CSRs. At the same time, consumers usually dread calling into customer support, even if the center is well run. It feels like an errand, and an unpleasant one at that. Complex phone trees, often ending with the caller repeatedly saying "representative," leave consumers with a bad taste in their mouths. A 2010 study in the *Harvard Business Review* observed, "Although customer service can do little to increase loyalty, it can (and typically does) do a great deal to undermine it. Customers are four times more likely to leave a service interaction disloyal than loyal." Even with cutbacks, most businesses continue to pay hundreds of millions of dollars to fund their customer support centers because they feel they have to.

In some respects, the call center is like the legal system: an important backstop for the tiny percentage of cases that require in-depth, in-person support, but no longer the best resolution channel for the vast majority of cases. No one wants to take time out of their day to sit on hold waiting for a customer service representative unless they really have no other choice.

Phantom "Customer Satisfaction"

The slogans read like motivational mantras: "Customer satisfaction is job one," "The customer is always right," and "We're not happy unless you're happy." Indeed, businesses relentlessly tout their attention to customer satisfaction and wallpaper their offices with posters saying exactly that. Companies purchase sophisticated systems to track user satisfaction regarding individual processes and flows, as well as their satisfaction regarding their overall relationship with the business. An industry-standard metric called the Net Promoter Score (NPS) is used by businesses across all of their customer interactions to track progress in improving satisfaction over time. Increasingly, however, businesses are discovering from close analysis of the data that satisfaction as measured through self-reported surveys is a very imprecise way to measure success.

The challenge is that satisfaction is often correlated directly with outcome, so users who get what they want in a particular interaction indicate that they are satisfied and users who do not get what they want are dissatisfied. Businesses often find that it is relatively easy to manipulate satisfaction numbers simply by automatically paying out more claims or "no faulting" cases so that no one loses. Those short-term changes might improve satisfaction and NPS scores for a limited period of time, but they are quite expensive and are not based on concrete changes in the underlying platform or service. As a result, the benefits to satisfaction disappear quickly once the payments stop.

A better indicator of a business relationship with a customer may be customer loyalty. Instead of relying on self-reported surveys to determine customer satisfaction, Internet businesses can examine user activity data to determine exactly how each user's behavior changes after they have a particular experience on the site. In many respects, this activity data may offer a better understanding of the user's satisfaction than user reports. A customer might say on a survey that a particular experience soured them on the site and they decreased their usage afterward, but the actual record of their use of the site or service tells the true story.

Rethinking Consumer Protection

If consumers do not want telephone-based customer support, what do they want? Again, it is clear: Consumers want resolution processes that work like the rest of their newly global, connected, online world. If the goal is to build a resolution system that is relevant to modern consumer expectations, the power of new technologies must be leveraged to meet the changing needs and expectations of customers. Consumers are impatient. They will give up if the process is laborious, slow, and antiquated. They want and expect resolutions to work the way the Internet works: fast, easy, fair, and effective.

This is where online dispute resolution (ODR) fits in. ODR offers a better blueprint for the evolution of consumer protection. Techniques such as negotiation, mediation, and arbitration do not require jurisdictional clarity in order to work. Even better, these approaches can be implemented in software so that issues can be addressed at any time, without making the consumer wait in a customer service queue or for a case to work its way through the courts. ODR fits with the expectations of modern disputants. Redress processes can be built directly into the online environments where transactions take place, and cases can be addressed and resolved in a matter of minutes and days instead of months or years.

Instead of the old process, which is laden with complex filing requirements and investigations, many consumers find it easier to communicate directly online with their merchant in an attempt to resolve problems by mutual agreement. If that approach does not work, the parties can easily invite a neutral third party to provide an expedited decision to resolve the case. These online processes may not have all the procedural protections of a court-based process or a formal arbitration; however, for many consumers, this "rough justice" is more than adequate to meet their needs. Again, they do not care about the legal niceties. They just want to get a resolution and move on—and that is what ODR empowers them to do.

Another advantage of ODR is that it is not limited to the current state of technology. There are sure to be plenty of breakthroughs waiting just around the bend, such as virtual reality, free in-browser high-definition video conferencing, or some other as-yet-undiscovered technology that will reinvent communication once again. ODR will immediately leverage these innovations as they become available and affordable. To predict the future utility of ODR based only on the current state of technology is to miss most of ODR's potential. It is not hard to envision a future where almost no consumers will be willing to pay the cost and suffer the inconvenience associated with an in-person meeting. Videoconferencing and online document exchange will be so high quality and omnipresent that online interaction will be the obvious preference. It is also not hard to envision a future where disputants prefer to interact textually and asynchronously instead of face-to-face to maximize efficiency and avoid unpleasant, annoying, and unproductive interactions.

Getting to the Heart of Consumers' Needs

In the July-August 2010 issue of the *Harvard Business Review*, Matthew Dixon, Karen Freeman, and Nicholas Toman shared the results of a massive consumer study by the Customer Contact Council, a division of the Corporate Executive Board. This study interviewed more than 75,000 consumers about their redress preferences and the conclusion was clear: "Corporate leaders must focus their service organizations on mitigating disloyalty by reducing customer effort." This study generated several conclusions that neatly summarize what modern consumers are looking for:

Consumers Want Fast and Easy Resolutions

Consumers in the digital age demand speed. A top priority for consumers is not having to spend a lot of effort to get their problems resolved. Poorly designed processes or excessively complex procedural requirements spike consumers' frustration. If a resolution process is overly prescriptive and time consuming, it will frustrate consumers and drive them away, even if it is fair. Many customers so prize efficiency that they would rather lose a dispute quickly than win a dispute after a long process. For low-dollar value transactions, it is simply not worth the headache to endure two weeks of trying to get an issue resolved. Even if consumers are eventually victorious and get a replacement item or a full refund, they still may leave the site because they just do not want to be inconvenienced again. As a Consumer Contact Council study concluded, "When it comes to service, companies create loyal customers primarily by helping them solve their problems quickly and easily."

Consumers Do Not Want to Pick Up the Telephone

Telephone-based customer support does not drive loyalty. As a Customer Contact Council study revealed,

> *[A] massive shift is under way in terms of customers' service preferences. Although most companies believe that customers overwhelmingly prefer live-phone service to self-service, our most recent data show that customers are, in fact, indifferent. This is an important tipping point and probably presages the end of phone-based service as the primary channel for customer service interactions.*

Some telephone-based support is probably required, but only as a last resort. Customers are frustrated when they have to pick up the phone to get an issue resolved. Phone support calls may harm—not help—satisfaction or loyalty. This is especially true when there is poor training in the call center.

Consumers Do Not Expect Perks and Giveaways

Customers generally are not motivated by perks and free giveaways. The Customer Contact Council survey made clear that most businesses should stop trying to "delight" their customers with over-the-top perks. Some businesses (e.g., fancy hotels, expensive restaurants) establish long-term relationships on the basis of these "delight" experiences. However, it is far more common for customers to punish companies with bad basic service than for customers to become loyal to companies as a result of some unexpected act of generosity. As the authors explain, "Loyalty has a lot more to do with how companies perform on their plain vanilla service, meeting their stated obligations, than their attention to delighting customers. Most companies don't understand this, and they pay dearly in terms of wasted money and lost customers." The *New Handshake* is about getting the basics right, not going above and beyond with unneeded generosity.

Consumers Do Not Want to Negotiate

Consumers do not want to fight for what they are entitled to. If everything is negotiable, it creates a sense that only the complainers get the best deals. Even if customers feel good about a deal, they still may have a nagging sense that an even better deal might have been possible if they had pushed harder. No customer wants to face confrontation. That only generates anxiety and irritation, not customer goodwill. It creates the conditions that lead to the squeaky wheel syndrome. Businesses must strive to give their customers the sense that they are partners in seeking solutions. Companies and consumers should be aligned in trying to get problems resolved quickly and fairly. Pushing consumers into negotiations where they have to fight for the best outcome emphasizes the consumer-versus-merchant dynamic, which runs directly counter to the spirit of the *New Handshake.*

Consumers Want To Be Treated Fairly

Consumers want to know that the solutions they achieve are consistent and reasonable. If there is a policy in place that (a) creates tiered pricing or differentiated resolutions or (b) requires multiple administrative steps to get to resolution in an attempt to urge consumers to give up, buyers will get annoyed. Outcomes need to be predictable, fair, and consistent in their application. In the age of the Internet, you can be sure that consumers will talk to each other and compare their outcomes. One may not ask the person next to him on an airplane what they paid for the flight, but you can bet that the person is checking websites and asking friends on Facebook what is the best price.

It is also important for businesses to realize that "fairness" often requires a full refund. It is short-sighted to assume that full refunds should be reserved for the squeakiest wheels. That is not to say that everyone deserves a refund. However, if you paid $100 for an item that has not arrived after two weeks, you should not have to wade through a long process of paper filings to get your $100 back. You have just wasted two weeks and have nothing to show for it. You did not get your item, and you are at the same place you were before the transaction ever took place.

Some businesses expect buyers to write them a thank-you note when they provide a refund to the consumer. It is true that getting your money back is better than losing your money, but neither is a big win and neither will drive consumer loyalty. A consumer may go through that experience and then decide never to shop at that online store again because that merchant wasted his or her time.

Consumers Want Their Privacy Protected

Another piece of the puzzle deserves consideration: Consumers also want businesses to protect their privacy. A survey by the law firm Morrison & Forester exploring attitudes on privacy found that nearly one in three U.S. consumers (35 percent) made a decision whether or not to purchase a product from a company because of privacy concerns. Furthermore, of the consumers who were concerned about privacy, 82 percent said that privacy has adversely affected purchasing a product or service—an increase of 28 percent from 2011. Therefore, privacy is a revenue issue. Indeed, businesses that suffer data breaches lose customers. Furthermore, the survey found that higher-income and higher-educated consumers are more likely to stop purchasing due to a breach. Moreover, when asked to explain why they are concerned about privacy, 52 percent of survey respondents cited identity theft as the primary concern, followed by "privacy is a right." Privacy is pivotal in the fairness equation.

The Takeaway

Fundamentally, customers want any issues they encounter to be fully resolved to their satisfaction as quickly and fairly as possible. The new ideal protection experience for a consumer is to visit an easily discoverable website or mobile app, click a few options to describe the situation, and then have the case automatically resolved through a secure portal. Even better is for the company itself to identify the problem, automatically resolve it, and then notify the customer. Speed, efficiency, ease of resolution, safety, and consistent fairness are the top priorities for consumers.

Many businesses have traditionally downplayed their resolution systems because they think that talking about problems with buyers will make them less likely to utilize the services of the website in question. Often, resolution processes are hidden deep inside help content or made available only to users who proactively contact the website to complain about a problem. This approach is in direct opposition to what modern consumers now want from the businesses they transact with.

Problem resolution is perhaps the most important loyalty moment for consumers. In e-commerce, transactions with no problems (i.e., the buyer purchases an item and it arrives without a hitch) is the default expectation—the table stakes for e-commerce, if you will. The loyalty moment comes when the buyer experiences something out of the ordinary. That is when the business is presented with an opportunity to step up, do the right thing, and make a lasting, positive impression on that customer.

Some e-commerce companies have understood this dynamic for many years. Those websites often provide very streamlined resolution processes to their buyers, along with very generous refunds and returns. Over time, those companies have claimed a greater share of the overall e-commerce marketplace. Amazon, the e-commerce company that has most consistently championed the consumer, now receives $0.51 of every $1 spent on e-commerce in the United States. Other e-commerce companies that have demonstrated a weaker commitment to consumer protection have seen their share of e-commerce activity fall in comparison to the companies that have put consumer protection front and center.

This is true for both products and services. Consider cell phone services and airlines, where failure to address consumer complaints leads to lost revenue and loyalty. Being upfront with customers about resolution systems and providing an excellent resolution experience once a problem crops up are essential to building loyalty with customers. Investments in fast and fair resolution systems generate real returns, which more than compensate for the expense of putting those systems in place. Proactive communications to customers and clients about resolutions is good business, and organizations that ignore or downplay resolutions do so at their own peril.

CHAPTER 3

Lessons Learned on eBay

Talking in the abstract about the challenges and expectations of modern consumers can only go so far. The new kinds of redress and protection programs that undergird the New Handshake *have already been launched, scaled, and tested by the big Internet intermediaries, first and foremost the global eBay marketplace. The lessons learned from eBay's experiences are helpful in understanding the evolution taking place in global consumer protection.*

In 2007, eBay was the largest e-commerce marketplace in the world and PayPal (eBay's wholly owned payments subsidiary) was the largest online payment company in the world. eBay sells billions of items per year; at any given moment, there are more than 100 million items for sale on the site. eBay users trade almost every kind of item imaginable in more than 50,000 categories. On eBay, a pair of shoes sells every 7 seconds, a cell phone sells every 7 seconds, and a car sells every 56 seconds. The daily volume of trade on eBay is greater than the daily volume of the NASDAQ. PayPal has 192 million active digital wallets and is available in 203 markets, supporting more than 100 different currencies. PayPal's total payment volume (the total value of transactions) in the fourth quarter of 2014 was $64.3 billion, meaning that PayPal transacted more than $485,000 in total payment volume every minute or more than 11.5 million payments every day.

As the first global online e-commerce platform, eBay was the earliest company in the world to have to solve some of the difficult problems associated with the creation and maintenance of a cross-jurisdictional, high-volume, low-value marketplace. When eBay launched, the biggest challenge was that consumers simply did not trust that they would get what they paid for. eBay quickly realized that without consumer trust, the system could not work. In response, eBay created the first Trust and Safety (TnS) team, which was tasked with ensuring the trustworthiness of the eBay ecosystem. Today, almost every e-commerce and marketplace company has a TnS team, but the concept was invented at eBay. Within TnS, there are three main divisions (the "three legs of the trust stool"): Fraud Investigations (for catching and punishing the bad guys), Feedback and Reputation (for creating transparency and sharing information with users), and Protections/Resolutions.

The main objective for TnS was maintaining trust within eBay, which is much harder than it sounds. Trust is a somewhat slippery concept. It exists entirely within the mind of the user. Some websites are trusted even though they should not be, and some websites are not trusted even though they are doing everything right. Major new initiatives that were launched to tackle specific trust issues within eBay sometimes did not move the trust needle very much, but a marketing campaign or prominent media story would move the trust needle quite a bit. Trust exists in the minds of the individuals who experience it. Therefore, using self-reported perceptions of trust as a way to measure the effectiveness of any trust-building efforts is not necessarily a good way to determine if you are on track.

At the beginning of eBay, the approach was more along the lines of a classified site: Create a bulletin board where buyers and sellers can find each other, then let the users handle their own affairs. If a buyer wanted to be risky and purchase from a seller with a mixed reputation and track record, so be it. Over time, eBay realized that, even with the information provided about the transaction histories of all the users, buyers could not effectively protect themselves from being taken advantage of without some help. The information asymmetry and repeat-player advantage of sellers was too great for buyers to overcome. The bad experiences of buyers in this "caveat emptor" marketplace were harming the perceived trustworthiness of the site. Thus, eBay evolved into a "managed marketplace," where eBay employees took on the responsibility to help buyers avoid bad experiences and resolve problems when they arose.

eBay and Resolutions

As you might imagine, these billions of purchases generated a lot of consumer issues. Even though only about 1 percent of purchases generated a problem, the incredible volume on eBay meant that eBay and PayPal handled more than 60 million disputes a year in more than 16 different languages. Depending on how you count, that daily volume is in excess of all civil filings in U.S. courts.

Building a resolution system for eBay was like building a civil justice system for a country. eBay's 250 million users, if counted as citizens, would have made eBay the fifth largest country in the world. In designing appropriate resolution and protection flows, it was important to consider all of the effects such a system would have across the entire global eBay marketplace.

eBay has now been on the front lines of online dispute resolution (ODR) for more than two decades. In fact, *The Perfect Store*, Adam Cohen's book about the early days of eBay, describes how dispute resolution was a part of eBay in the first months after Pierre Omidyar launched the site in his San José basement in 1995. As Cohen explained, eBay's first customer support employee, Uncle Griff, "spent a lot of time doing what Omidyar hated: stepping in and trying to resolve disputes."

In 1999, Professor Ethan Katsh launched a pilot program with eBay to resolve disagreements between buyers and sellers. After a link was put on a relatively obscure eBay help page urging people to report issues, Katsh's Online Ombuds Center at the University of Massachusetts Amherst was flooded with cases. That pilot program evolved into a startup company, SquareTrade.com, which in turn grew to become the web's most successful online mediation service. Over the next four years, SquareTrade mediators would resolve several million eBay disputes. However, there were many other types of disputes that SquareTrade could not address as an independent, third-party service provider outside of the eBay ecosystem. As a result, eBay made the decision to bring ODR in-house in 2003.

Characteristics of eBay Disputes

eBay has a wide variety of disputes, and each type is fraught with its own specific complexities. Some disputes are initiated by sellers (e.g., payment disputes), whereas others are initiated by buyers (e.g., item quality disputes). Some disputes focus on reputation (feedback disputes) and others on intellectual property (owner rights disputes). Most of these disputes are not over very large amounts of money. They can be for as little as $5, such as a magazine, or as much as $50,000, such as a car, but the average is around $100. However, as dispute resolvers know well, dollar amount is usually not an accurate barometer of passion among disputants. Also, because eBay users are spread all over the world, eBay disputes can involve cultural misunderstandings, language barriers, and class differences.

Clearly, the top challenge for eBay's ODR system is the overwhelming volume of cases. With tens of millions of disputes, the math was obvious: Even if eBay had built a staff of 10,000 skilled online mediators, it would be impossible to get through the torrent of cases. At the time, eBay had a total of 25,000 employees around the world. It was self-evident that the process needed to be as automated as possible.

Designing an ODR System for eBay

It was clear to everyone in TnS that the best path forward would be to write a software program to assist the parties in resolving their disputes and to involve human neutrals only on an exceptional basis. The question was how to do it. No one had ever built a system to handle such high volumes of cases.

eBay's advantage in resolutions lay in the fact that eBay was not a party in each individual transaction. As the marketplace administrator, eBay was a credible neutral third party in any transaction problem. eBay was also in direct communication with the buyer and seller from the very beginning, from the purchase all the way through to resolution. Additionally, eBay had absolute enforcement power because eBay could move money from one party to the other through PayPal. That enabled eBay to immediately connect with both parties, freeze the funds in question pending the outcome, and ensure that resolutions could be immediately enforced.

One crucial factor was eBay's ability to work with the parties even before they really understood whether they had a problem. For instance, if a buyer made a purchase and the item had not arrived within three or four days, he or she might start to get concerned. eBay could then step in to reassure the buyer that the average delivery time for a package going from the seller's location to the buyer's home was seven days. Then the buyer's anxiety would ease, and the package would later arrive on schedule. In a sense, eBay was able to resolve the issue before it even became a dispute.

There was also an upside to the incredible volume of disputes coming through eBay's systems. eBay knew an immense amount about the types of problems that occurred on the site because so many of them had already come through the system. eBay's data warehouse was filled with millions of records that could be used to better understand what was going on. It was very rare to see a wholly new kind of dispute. Such familiarity with the full spectrum of issues within the marketplace enabled the design of dedicated and automated systems tailored specifically to each dispute type.

For example, most item-related disputes fell into one of two categories: nonreceipt (the buyer paid but never got anything) or not as described (the item arrived but was different than what the buyer expected). Then, within these dispute types, further questions could pinpoint the problem: How did the seller ship the item? Was shipping insurance purchased? In the case of a not-as-described item, was the item broken? Was it counterfeit? Was the difference a small one (e.g., wrong color) or a big one (e.g., the buyer bought a new laptop and got an old, broken one instead)?

The language used on the site also had to promote resolution. "Fraud alerts" became "item not received" disputes. A "Dispute Console" made the tracking and resolution of problems much easier. The console enabled users to see all of their transaction problems in one place, communicate easily with their transaction partners, and track them to resolution. Soon after, community members began using this language to talk about their transaction problems in the discussion forums. Several years later, the Dispute Console turned into the Resolution Center. The language used helped to change the way users thought about consumer problems on eBay, increasing the likelihood of resolution.

Building a Framework for ODR

In designing the framework for the eBay dispute resolution system, it was vital to design a process that would resolve every issue reported. A purely facilitative model that left the outcome up to the parties would generate a lot of frustration. It would leave many of the toughest cases unresolved. Also, some parties had an interest in not reaching an agreement (for instance, a seller in the case of a not-as-described dispute). In such a case, a party, usually the seller, simply does not want to pay. The party therefore has a strong incentive to stonewall or refuse to negotiate in good faith.

Accordingly, the ODR framework for eBay took a staircase design. It began with problem diagnosis and working directly with the complainant, then escalated to direct negotiation assisted by technology, and finally moved to an evaluation phase where eBay would decide the case if the transaction partners could not do so. Each party could decide unilaterally when it wanted the process to move on to the next phase. The goal of the system was to prevent as many disputes as possible, amicably resolve as many as possible, and then decide the remainder as quickly and fairly as possible. Each stage acted like a filter, with the objective being to minimize the flow of cases that made it to the end.

It was very clear that eBay users did not want to spend a lot of time in extensive processes intended to build a long-term trustworthy relationship. Most eBay transactions were between strangers and most buyers did not buy more than one item from any individual seller. Thus there was little interest in approaches that did not match this purely transactional orientation. What users wanted was communication, transparency, efficiency, and a fair outcome, in as little time as possible. The priorities were speed, minimizing effort, and fairness.

eBay discussed filing fees for their dispute processes because the mediations through SquareTrade had required filing fees. However, it is difficult to convince a disputant to pay $30 to resolve a $50 dispute, and nearly impossible to convince him or her to pay $50 to resolve a $50 dispute. The disputant might as well just give the money to the other side and save the time associated with the process. Moving ODR inside eBay was a much more natural way to address the funding problem. Instead of thinking about the costs on a per-case basis, as one does with a third-party provider, eBay evaluated the cost for the system on a revenue-enablement basis, which made much more economic sense. Extensive economic analysis was conducted to determine the cost-benefit ratio of the resolution program. The analysis demonstrated clearly that the savings from reduced contacts with customer service, improved loyalty from users, and increased transaction activity more than justified the investments in ODR.

From the beginning, eBay's ODR processes were designed to be learning systems. There was no shortage of data available; eBay has total visibility into each user's usage patterns, history, and account data. Also, eBay routinely surveys users to get their feedback on the resolution processes they have used. eBay uses these data to monitor the performance of their systems and improve them as marketplace conditions change.

Aiming for 100 Percent Automation: Payment Disputes

The biggest volume of disputes at eBay had to do with nonpayment. The issue of consumers bidding on items and not following through to pay was causing great consternation in the marketplace. The system in place to deal with those issues was very manual. Sellers were quite upset at what they saw as eBay taking money from them for no reason because buyers never followed through and paid. At the annual eBay Live! Conference, there were sessions with hundreds of angry sellers expressing great aggravation with the existing processes. Consumers were frustrated as well by the nontransparent way they were penalized for nonpayment.

On eBay, sellers paid two times when they sold an item. They paid a small insertion fee to list the item and then a small "final value fee" when the item was purchased. The final value fee was based on the final sales price. Therefore, a seller may list a Ferrari on eBay and a teenager may bid on the car as a joke with a very high amount. When the auction closes, the seller thinks the item is sold, even though the buyer will never follow through and pay. eBay charges the seller the final value fee as soon as the item closes based on the sales price. The seller then has to wait for the buyer to follow through and pay. If the buyer does not pay, the seller is still out the fee paid to eBay.

eBay users informally called this process the "deadbeat bidder" process. In official documents, it was called the "nonpaying bidder" process. The language used to describe the process went a long way toward defining how users thought of it. eBay concluded that the name of the process had to change because it is never wise to name the process something that indicates who is at fault (in this case, the bidder) and possibly even insults them (in the case of "deadbeat"). There are legitimate reasons for a buyer not to follow through and pay for an item they committed to buy on eBay—perhaps a seller changed the shipping price after the auction closed or refused to include a component that was advertised in the original listing. In these cases, the buyer should not actually follow through and pay, and as such does not deserve to be called a deadbeat.

Sellers were aggrieved because they felt that eBay should not be profiting off of transactions that were not completed. They felt the process to receive reimbursements for final value fees was overly onerous with lots of hidden deadlines, which maximized the chance that sellers would miss their filing windows and give up on trying to get refunds. They also felt that they should not receive feedback from buyers who did not follow through and pay for items they had purchased. The sellers' rationale was that if the buyer did not complete the transaction by paying, then they should not have the right to leave a public comment on the seller's profile.

The first change that eBay made was to rename the flow as the "unpaid item (UPI) process." Although this may seem relatively trivial, translating a new name into 16 languages around the world and updating thousands of help pages is not a minor task. Second, eBay designed a new system for managing UPI cases. This new system was designed from inception to be technology only. No human customer service representatives would be required to work with the buyer and seller in order to resolve the issue.

The UPI process had a fairly simple flow. The seller would come to the Dispute Console and report an item as unpaid by entering in the item number.

The buyer would then be notified of the new case and was asked to respond. When a buyer responded to the dispute, he or she had several response options:

1. I have already paid for this item.
2. I would like to pay for this item now.
3. I do not want to pay for this item.

The seller then had the ability to respond to the buyer. Each side could post messages in the joint discussion. The seller had the unilateral ability to end the discussion at any point and give the buyer an unpaid item strike. If the buyer received too many unpaid item strikes in too short a period of time, then their account would be suspended.

Buyers and sellers could also cancel the transaction by mutual agreement. If the seller indicated that he or she was willing to release the buyer from his or her obligation to purchase the item and the buyer indicated that he or she agreed to the cancellation as well, then the purchase was cancelled in the eBay system. The seller received his or her reimbursement, and no action was taken against the buyer.

The only human involvement in the UPI process was when a buyer appealed an unpaid item strike. The buyer filled out a form explaining why he or she thought the strike was received in error, and a customer service representative evaluated the information submitted in order to make a decision. What the buyer did not know was that all first appeals from buyers are granted automatically, so only the second appeal is actually reviewed by a person. This means that a caseload of more than 30 million cases per year can run automatically, requiring only a couple thousand manual reviews per year.

Originally, any buyer who received three strikes was thrown off of the system. However, some high-volume buyers (e.g., professional buyers) said that this arbitrary number was unfair because they engaged in so many more transactions and it created jeopardy for them in their account. Eventually, the policy was changed so that buyers were thrown off of eBay if they received too many UPI strikes in too short a period of time. That gave eBay the flexibility to adjust the criteria based on a buyer's transaction volume.

Combatting Gaming

One consistent concern in all of eBay's ODR flows was gameability. Because there were millions of users working through the UPI process, there were plenty of attempts from individuals to find ways to exploit the system. As soon as any new flow was launched publicly, there were users who would test it out from every angle, looking to see if there was a way to take advantage of it.

For example, a major concern at eBay was a problem called "shill bidding." This happens when a user lists an item under one account and then logs in as a second account to bid up the price on the item. eBay had advanced technology in place to catch any sellers who tried something like this, as was often discovered by a casual seller who bid on his own item from his wife's account or from the same IP address. eBay has zero tolerance for shill bidding, and sellers who were found engaging in it were immediately thrown off the site. This happened to some very large sellers, at great expense to eBay.

Shill bidders would occasionally win their own items, which of course they did not want to follow through with. The UPI process was part of shill bidding because if the seller could not get his or her final value fee refunded, shill bidding was a losing proposition. Shill bidding was a problem that could not be tolerated without a significant reduction in trust, so the UPI process had to help catch the bad actors. Because the UPI process was entirely automated, it was important that it be highly impervious to this type of gaming. Checks and reports were built into the UPI process to help eBay find this kind of abusive behavior. Verification steps from buyers and sellers were also added to make automation of this process impossible.

Lessons Learned

Now that the systems built at eBay have processed hundreds of millions of disputes, much has been learned about what modern consumers expect in terms of resolutions and protections. These lessons have helped eBay to validate the conclusions from the prior chapter around what consumers really want. Although the scope of lessons learned at eBay is wide, for the purposes of the *New Handshake* we can summarize the key ones in 10 main areas, which emphasize many of the points previously discussed in Chapter 2.

Resolutions Should Be Fast and Easy

The lesson learned again and again by eBay was that users just want the marketplace to work. The consumer relationship with eBay is very straightforward: I buy it, you get it to me, and we are good. If a problem arises, consumers want to get it resolved quickly and easily so that they do not have to waste time worrying about it. In that sense, consumer resolutions are kind of like the dentist's office: No one walks around all day thinking about how much he or she loves the dentist's office (except maybe dentists). However, if you have a toothache, all you can think about is getting to the dentist's office. Once the toothache is gone, you walk out the door and do not think about the dentist any more. Resolutions and protections are there to solve a problem. When buyers need this help, they want it to work quickly and effectively so that they can put the issue to bed and get on with their lives. That is what success looks like.

In retrospect, the early frustration with disputes on eBay was not a problem of policy; rather, it was a problem of complexity. Without a console to track issues and a simple process for getting them worked out, resolving problems was too hard. That was what most annoyed eBay users. The issue was not the outcomes achieved so much as the difficulty of the process required to achieve the outcomes. Once eBay built an easy-to-use hub for managing problems and a clear process that tracked every matter to closure, the frustration went away.

Discoverability and Easy Access Are Very Important

Before eBay created the Resolution Center, the fastest way to access the filing form for a new matter (then called the "fraud alert") was seven not-very-obvious clicks from the homepage. Even if that program had been well designed, it would not have mattered much because no one could find it. Once the process was improved and rebranded as the Resolution Center, links to it were added to the top and bottom of every page on the site. Prominent links were also placed on the "Items I've Purchased" page for every user, enabling them to report a problem with a single click. These changes increased the overall volume of problems reported, which initially caused concern. However, these issues had always existed—eBay just had not known about them before because reporting them had been too onerous. Over time, eBay realized that it was a good thing to know about these issues because then eBay could help resolve them, which improved buyer loyalty. If eBay did not know about the problem, the buyer would suffer in silence, likely leaving eBay and never coming back.

As it turns out, because the software built to automate resolutions was so effective, the net number of disputes that had to be worked by a customer service representative decreased. This was true although the total number of reported cases increased significantly. Now, eBay almost begs consumers to report problems because the data have demonstrated so conclusively that problem resolution is such a powerful way to build loyalty—even more effective than promotions, marketing, or high-touch customer service.

Consumers Are Not Motivated by Giveaways

Some people at eBay argued that less time should be spent on resolving problems, and consumers should just be paid off every time they encountered a problem. For a time, this perspective held sway, and the approach was put into practice. Hundreds of millions of dollars were spent providing instant refunds, gift card incentives, and eBay-branded giveaways. Users were always surprised when these unexpected presents arrived and they were polite in communicating their thanks, but the data were very clear that these initiatives did not build customer loyalty or increased transaction activity. Plus, these initiatives were enormously expensive. The individuals who advanced this approach are no longer working at eBay.

Satisfaction Is Not a Good Way to Measure the Effectiveness of Resolutions Programs

We found that it was nearly impossible to evaluate the success of our efforts based on self-reported satisfaction surveys. eBay users would sometimes insist up and down that a certain new feature would massively improve their satisfaction; however, when eBay launched it, it had little effect. Conversely, eBay would launch a new feature that users previously indicated they were indifferent about, but which generated a major increase in satisfaction. Finally, users often misreported how satisfied they were or how that satisfaction affected their usage of our site. They might say they were going to close their account and never come back as the result of a bad experience, but they were back on the site two days later, using the services more than they had ever used them before. It was very difficult to use satisfaction metrics to guide strategic decision making because they were often so disconnected from reality. Also, as previously mentioned, user perceptions of trust on the site seemed more correlated to marketing campaigns than site functionality. eBay had to find other metrics that gave a better idea of the real impact of their initiatives (such as loyalty and reactivation).

Sellers Have the Advantage

It is important to design resolution flows that are cognizant of the structural advantages enjoyed by sellers. These advantages do not mean that sellers are doing anything wrong or that they are necessarily exploiting their buyers. It simply means that the additional experience and information enjoyed by sellers does not provide a level playing field with buyers if a problem arises.

As a systems designer for e-commerce resolution systems, it is always easier to listen to sellers than it is to listen to buyers. Sellers make their living in the marketplace, so they are there every day. They track every change in policy and know who to contact if they are unhappy about something. If you hold a big conference and invite buyers and sellers, 95 percent of the people who show up will be sellers, because a) they are willing to spend the money to attend, and b) they have a bigger financial stake in the future of the marketplace than do the buyers.

The voices of consumers are harder to hear. There are many more buyers, but they are not as organized. They do not follow every development within the marketplace assiduously because they may be buying in a variety of different environments. They do not know who to call if they encounter a problem. However, their voices are just as important, if not more important, than those of the sellers. eBay found that if you have the buyers (e.g., the demand), the sellers will appear. If you have the sellers (e.g., the supply), the buyers will not necessarily come—unless they trust that they will have a good experience and that problems will be quickly resolved.

You Have Got to Set the Right Tone

Language matters, particularly in an environment where everyone is interacting asynchronously, via online text, and never meeting face-to-face. The language used to describe the issues that arise and the tools that are available to resolve those issues must frame the matters in a way that promotes reason and resolution. If the framing instead warns of fraud, deception, and chicanery, it will be that much harder to craft agreement.

eBay found that the first message posted in a thread really sets the tone for the conversation from there on out. If the first message has a negative tone, then the tone of the overall thread is usually negative. It was the rare message thread that started out negative and then had the tone turn around. Usually, there was one message posted by the seller or buyer that asked to reset the tone of the communication and improve it. Maybe the item arrived and the buyer admitted to overreacting, or the seller apologized and took responsibility. However, usually when the first message was aggressive, the whole discussion thread would be aggressive.

The challenge is that the buyer is usually the complainant in item-related disputes, and the buyer is usually frustrated. Buyers also have little incentive to be reasonable. Buyers do not care about negative feedback or bad reviews; there is no financial downside for buyers who receive negative feedback.

As a result, eBay structured the resolution process so that the first post from the buyer was intermediated by technology. The buyer filled out a series of very comprehensive forms where they picked the reason for their dispute. From these selections, eBay could compose a first post for them that accurately described the nature of their complaint but avoided any threats or insults. The buyer was not given an open text box to explain their situation because of the risk that they would use that opportunity to sling accusations at the seller.

The seller, on the other hand, had great incentives to resolve the case amicably. If a seller got negative feedback, that might serve to reduce the willingness of future buyers to make purchases from him. It also might besmirch the seller in the eyes of eBay. The seller already had the ideal outcome for the transaction: He or she had the money and the buyer had the item. If the payment was reversed, then the seller would be annoyed. Therefore, sellers have a very strong incentive to work out the problem. As such, eBay gave sellers the first opportunity to post an open message because they were likely to set a positive tone. This kind of artful system design can be very helpful in maximizing the number of transaction problems resolved through mutual agreement.

Do Not Presume Everything Is Fraud

One of the core values at eBay is the belief that people are good. In some respects, eBay can be viewed as a giant sociological experiment testing that proposition. By any objective standard, it must be concluded that the hypothesis is true: People are good, at least the vast majority of the time. eBay has facilitated billions of transactions where one stranger sends money to another stranger on the promise that the second stranger will follow through with his or her obligation. Most of the time, it works without a hitch.

However, it is human nature to see malevolent intentions in others even when no such malevolent intentions exist. This kind of fundamental attribution error plays out every day within the eBay marketplace—the "people are good" value notwithstanding. When an item does not arrive, consumers are often very quick to jump to the conclusion that their seller is a fraudster who is looking to play them for a fool. In fact, after observing hundreds of millions of cases, the vast majority of transaction problems are misunderstandings—the item was delivered next door by accident, the husband received the package from the delivery man and put it in the garage without telling the wife, or the seller forgot to take the box to the post office and it is still sitting in his or her trunk. Healthy marketplaces like eBay see a small percentage of their transactions generate some sort of problem, but only a fraction of those problems are fraud. The vast majority of problems are misunderstandings, usually the result of human mistakes or inefficiency. It does not make sense to build resolution systems that presume ill intent in most cases.

Outcomes Have to Be Consistent and Fair

Sellers were convinced that the eBay resolution process was biased toward buyers, and buyers were convinced that the eBay resolution process was biased toward sellers. In a complex resolution ecosystem like eBay, that may be as close as you can reasonably get to a level playing field. eBay users posted endless messages in the discussion forums comparing the outcomes they got from the various resolutions processes on the site. Buyers and sellers were constantly checking with each other to see if the policies on eBay were being enforced consistently and discussing what seemed fair or unfair.

This is one of the problems with automatic refunds in isolation. If a buyer files a dispute in an online marketplace and gets an immediate reimbursement, that is good. However, the question remains: What will ensure that this does not happen again to other buyers? Is the marketplace simply paying off buyers who experience problems but not addressing the causes of those problems? Buyers want to know that their resolution will have ramifications beyond just their specific case. If a consumer feels that the reimbursement is just papering over problems in the marketplace, he or she may feel encouraged to engage in buyer fraud, thinking that if it is easy to click a button and get an instant reimbursement without any questions asked, the incentives to overreport problems is strong.

To a certain extent, it is more important that the outcomes be consistent than fair. Fairness can very much be in the eye of the beholder. Supreme Court Justice Oliver Wendell Holmes was known for expressing his distaste for the title "Justice" because he thought that justice was too high a standard. Justice was meted out by God, he argued; his job was to interpret the law. eBay could not ensure that every user was given exactly what they deserved in every exchange. However, eBay could create policies and processes that consistently administered the publicly displayed rules, and the confidence that resulted from that consistency was a powerful bulwark to trust.

Resolution Processes Do Not Need to Be Binding

The UNCITRAL Working Group spent an inordinate amount of time on a simple, fundamental disagreement: whether the outcomes of the ODR process should be legally binding. The U.S. delegation argued that they should (in line with the *Concepcion* decision rendered by the Supreme Court), and the European Union steadfastly opposed the idea. Endless hours of negotiating were devoted to this particular disagreement. Despite over six years of discussions, it was never resolved. From the eBay perspective, this question is moot. The courts were and are irrelevant to most eBay consumers and merchants. No court wants to hear a case over a $75 eBay purchase, and no lawyer wants to take that case, especially when the transaction might cross borders.

The eBay resolution process did not explicitly block customer redress in a court. Users always had the ability to escalate their case by filing it in another channel, whether that was a credit card chargeback, an advocacy organization (e.g., the Better Business Bureau), a state consumer protection authority, or the courts. Because users trust the eBay process, the matters are almost never pursued beyond the eBay resolution flows. If consumers and merchants trust a resolution process to be fair, consistent, transparent, and easy to use, then they do not require an additional layer of redress. Additionally, eBay has the ability to immediately enforce any outcomes achieved, so there was no reason to rely upon the courts for enforcement. The eBay experience demonstrates that private resolution mechanisms can be wholly effective without relying on the legal system in any way.

Resolution Systems Need to Be Continuously Learning

Because eBay had so much volume coming into the system, the company was rarely surprised by a new dispute filing. They had pretty much seen every kind of dispute before. However, there were circumstances where eBay learned something about disputes that urged them to reform the upstream processes.

One good example is return-related disputes. In a large number of cases, the buyer and seller disagreed over item returns. Maybe the buyer said he wanted to return the item after the seller's specified return window. Maybe the seller charged a restocking fee or refunded the buyer in store credit instead of cash. In most cases, the seller insisted that the buyer pay for return shipping, and the buyer was not happy about it. When a buyer received an item that she thought was inaccurately described in the listing, she felt that she should be able to return it and get all her money back. Sellers usually disagreed because they were out the shipping price on the original item purchase, and they were not excited about having to pay shipping again.

eBay realized that the best way to tackle these disputes was not after they arose, but upstream in the process. So they took their learnings and went to the "Sell Your Item" team, who owned the form that sellers used to list their items for sale on the site. Working with that team, a listing feature was added to capture return information in a much more detailed fashion. Sellers could specify their return window, how they delivered returns, and whether or not they would cover return shipping. eBay also raised the profile of this information in the listing view, so buyers would be aware of it when they were deciding to make a purchase. As a result, there was a big drop off in the volume of dispute filings related to returns disputes.

Online consumer resolution systems must be constantly learning from the cases flowing through the system and updating the rules and processes accordingly. No ODR solution is perfect right out of the box. Instead, every process must evolve with the marketplace. Without this layer of continuous feedback, an effective resolution process may slowly get out of sync with the needs of consumers and become less and less effective over time.

Takeaways

The global eBay marketplace is as huge as it is pioneering. The company tackled many trust-related challenges for the first time and learned a lot from those experiences. However, eBay always knew this was only one part of the e-commerce elephant. There were other marketplaces and merchants growing bigger than eBay, particularly in Asia, and there was an even bigger segment of overall transaction volume that was being processed directly through websites that merchants put up themselves, with no overarching marketplace administrator ensuring consumer protection or fair resolutions. It was obvious that at some point the lessons learned at eBay would have to be applied to a much larger systems-design exercise—one that looked at global e-commerce as a whole instead of thinking only about the transactions within our particular walled garden. That was the bigger challenge, and that is what the *New Handshake* is designed to address.

PART 2

Businesses, Consumer Advocates, and Ethics

CHAPTER 4

The Business Case for Resolutions

Businesses have traditionally been reluctant to proactively talk about providing resolutions for consumers with disputes or complaints about the businesses' products or services. However, the data tell a different story. In fact, resolutions are one of the top loyalty drivers for consumers. The dynamics of the Internet reward businesses that build trust with their consumers. Thus, businesses that provide fast and fair resolutions enjoy a significant competitive advantage.

Why do people start businesses? Most businesspeople are motivated by a sincere desire to generate value in the eyes of their customers and to build a successful and prosperous enterprise that is driven by that value. Seen from one angle, all businesses are about shortening distances. If you want a sweater, you can certainly buy a sheep, shear its wool, make the wool into yarn, and knit it yourself—but that is a heck of a lot of work for a sweater. Thanks to the magic of the marketplace, for a modest price, plenty of businesses will happily shorten the distance between you and the sweater, letting you spend your time on *Candy Crush* instead of herding sheep and cleaning out the barn. This is true for tangible items (e.g., a sweater) as well as services (e.g., having someone build you a website). When capitalism works right, both the business and the consumer are happy.

No one starts a business because they are excited about resolving consumer purchase or transaction problems. Most businesses are optimized around the vast majority of transactions that go smoothly, not the small percentage of transactions that generate problems. In fact, many new businesspeople are annoyed when transaction problems first emerge. Resolving problems feels like a distraction from the fun, profitable part of running a business. If you are a carpenter, you love making furniture, not arguing with your customer about whether the table you delivered is smaller than originally described. Some businesses work great for the 98 percent of transactions that go smoothly but still fail because of the 2 percent that run off of the rails. For that reason, many businesspeople find dealing with transaction problems quite frustrating.

The truth is that problems are inevitable. Even the best businesses in the world encounter problems. When a book is delivered, a husband may accept it from the delivery person and put it on the bookshelf without telling his wife—and the wife later files an item not received complaint. Maybe a baker accidentally puts nutmeg in a carrot cake after the consumer specifically told the person taking the order that they did not want nutmeg. Maybe the beautiful new logo for McDougal Motor Company has to be redone because, in fact, the name is MacDougal and no one thought to get the exact spelling over the phone. No matter what business you are in, unforeseen issues will always arise. They are part of the imperfect world in which we live.

Worse yet, problems engender frustration. Many people cannot resist the temptation to leap to conclusions and ascribe malevolent intentions to the other side when conflict arises. We are too quick to assume the baker put nutmeg in the cake as part of a passive-aggressive plot against the consumer. Likewise, the baker may be quick to blame the consumer for failing to mention the nutmeg when placing the order (instead of considering that the young employee taking the order dropped the ball). It is part of human nature to fundamentally misattribute bad intentions to others while maintaining benevolent interpretations of our own motivations. This truism of social psychology is easily observable in every corner of the Internet. In reality, the vast majority of transaction problems encountered by consumers are the result of miscommunication, misfortune, and benevolent sloppiness.

There is a stereotype that suggests businesses are so ruthlessly focused on profits that they will always seek ways to take advantage of their consumers. Some even suggest that a *majority* of businesses have this exploitative orientation. Although there are some bad actors out there, they are actually the exceptions to the rule. eBay found that transactions associated with bad actors accounted for less than one-tenth of 1 percent of the overall volume in the global marketplace, while total reported transaction problems were about 2 percent of transactions. The rate of buyer fraud was even lower. Although the stereotypes can urge us to conclude that everyone is operating in bad faith, the data tell a different story.

The vast majority of businesses want to take care of their customers. They want to do the right thing. Businesses seek to resolve problems fairly and efficiently, minimizing cost and churn in their business. This allows businesses to get back to the fun part: making profits and doing what they love.

A New Model for Business: The Sharing Economy

One of the more interesting phenomena engendered by the Internet is the degree to which the line between consumers and merchants has been blurred. Some new transaction platforms, often referred to as sharing or collaborative economy businesses, really are examples of consumers teaming up to deliver services to other consumers. These businesses are often structured in such a fashion that they are optimized entirely around consumer experience and consumer expectations. These businesses are designed from inception to be owned by the consumers and to operate exactly the way consumers want them to operate. In fact, many of the "merchants" are consumers themselves (think of sites such as eBay, AirBNB, Lyft, TaskRabbit, and others).

These types of businesses may be beacons of consumer protection in many cases, although they also may run afoul of fairness. Nonetheless, the aspiration is that these businesses operate almost like consumer empowerment organizations. Consumers are eager to utilize these sharing platforms because they feel like they are transacting with their peers. There is no sense of merchant versus consumer because the entire business is a community of consumers. The line between a buyer and a seller is extremely fuzzy. The responsibility of the administrator is to maintain a transparent and safe environment, with no bias toward the consumer or merchant. The only bias should be toward fairness and the continued health of the marketplace.

Over time, e-commerce is likely to shift further into these consumer-optimized marketplaces. Traditional merchants will even remake themselves to look more like collaborative economy companies. Because consumers have the easy ability to switch which marketplace they decide to purchase from, they are increasingly choosing the marketplaces where they feel they get the best support and easiest resolutions.

Currently, sharing economy companies are leading the way. In fact, when transacting in these consumer-driven collaborative economy environments, consumers do not expect "delight" experiences where they are given value above and beyond what they were promised. Instead, consumers feel more like they are members of a collective, where all of the marketplace participants agree to meet their responsibilities in good faith. In these types of transactions, problems and misunderstandings can still arise. However, because of the orientation of the business, platitudes like "the customer is always right" seem like a relic. Instead, all participants work on a level playing field. They have the obligation of being reasonable with each other. Bad actors in these environments are identified quickly and strongly incentivized to change their behavior. If they do not change, they are quickly ejected. Either play fair or you will be out of the game.

Making the Case for Investing in Resolutions

Managing a business is no simple task. It requires laser-like focus on competitive threats, profit and loss, and agile execution. A for-profit business is not a charity, so strategic decisions should not be based on hunches and personal preferences. Business leaders must continuously decide where to invest always-too-scarce resources and development days. To help with prioritization, each new project proposal is often subject to a cost-benefit analysis to determine the net-present value of following through with the initiative. If the cost to complete the project exceeds the projected financial benefits (either from increased revenues or cost savings), the project has a weak business case and is unlikely to be funded.

Many people think of dispute resolution as a self-evident good. Why do we resolve disputes? Because disputes are frustrating and annoying, so we should work them out as quickly as possible. For a business, however, that answer is not adequate. There is no doubt that consumers dislike disputes. However, if building a system to resolve them is too expensive or if disputes do not significantly dim the economic prospects of the business, then it might not make sense to invest resources in trying to resolve them.

The dispute resolution field has long struggled to quantitatively demonstrate the benefit of its work. Many studies have shown that dispute resolution services often receive very high satisfaction scores from users, and that users expect that any problems they encounter should be quickly addressed. However, the difficulty has been in demonstrating that this improved satisfaction generates concrete and replicable economic benefit. This hurdle has made arguing for continued investment in resolution systems quite difficult. Several high-quality dispute resolution programs have fallen victim to budget cuts because they were unable to justify continued expenditure on their operations from a purely cost-benefit analysis.

Calculating Return on Resolutions

To convince business leaders that resolutions should be a priority, the case must be made in dollars and cents. We refer to this analysis as *return on resolutions* (RoR). The way to calculate a true RoR is to view resolutions from a holistic perspective, integrating all-in costs, customer support, buyer retention and loyalty, and increased trust. Before the Internet, making these calculations was extremely complicated because there was no way to get access to all the data that were required. Now, however, large Internet companies are capturing incredible amounts of information that can help to get the full picture. For the first time, we can compute an all-in RoR metric that quantifies the economic benefit to companies that invest in building fast and fair resolution systems as a means of cultivating consumer trust.

A simple way to think about the potential RoR for a business is to calculate the true cost on a per-case basis of providing a resolution to a consumer. Sometimes, these calculations can be surprising to business leaders because costs are distributed around an organization, which leads them to be underestimated. There is not only the cost of the actual reimbursement to the consumer, but there is also the cost associated with the customer support representatives who have to spend the time communicating with the consumer and achieving closure. There are also costs associated with shipping, software, restocking, shrinkage, chargebacks, and repair. When all of these costs are fully considered, each individual case may cost a business upwards of $20 or $30 to resolve. Through that lens, any extended negotiation with the consumer just compounds the expense, potentially to the degree that the costs exceed the value of the item in question. Analyses like these often lead businesses to conclude that they should be much more generous with their automated refund policies.

As was discussed in the previous chapter, modern consumers crave fast and easy resolutions. Being able to leverage algorithms to deliver immediate case closure provides such resolutions while saving costs for the businesses. This is a true win-win for all parties involved. The merchant saves money while simultaneously delivering the experience the consumer wants. The strongest business case, therefore, is to leverage the power of software algorithms to resolve as many cases as possible without requiring a customer service representative to be involved. Most businesses have relatively rudimentary systems in place to deal with problems reported by their consumers, and often those processes are quite manual and dependent upon human customer service representatives to achieve closure in every case. eBay had 2,400 yearly disputes for every individual employee in the company. eBay's ODR was successful because the automated resolution rate reached 90 percent. That meant that 90 percent of the 60 million disputes were resolved in software only, not requiring any time or attention from customer service representatives. Similarly, the Resolution Center at PayPal saved the company more than $7.5 million in head count costs in the first year alone, and each year after that the savings compounded. When you add in the reduction in required protection payments, that is a powerful start for a business case.

The eBay experience demonstrates that the greatest RoR leverage occurs when policies and business rules autoresolve problems. Building the software that enables these policy-based resolutions can be complex and expensive, but fortunately there are prebuilt platforms available that can deliver this functionality at a much lower price point than building it from scratch.

Quantifying the Loyalty Benefit

Cost savings are one important consideration, but the real leverage in calculating RoR comes from increased consumer loyalty. It is difficult for a business to grow just by saving money. The better way to grow is to bring in new customers, and to get more business from the customers you already have. The difficult part is showing how a fast and fair resolution process impacts customer loyalty and retention. However, if your data set is robust and rich enough, you can get pretty close to definitive answers. Fortunately, eBay had just such a data set.

eBay's data warehouse contains almost a hundred petabytes of data. To get a sense of that scale, one petabyte is equivalent to 2,000 years of mp3-encoded music, 13.3 years of high-definition video, or all of the content in the U.S. Library of Congress multiplied by 50. eBay also has advanced tools to help analyze all that data in real time. Every click on the site is saved in the data warehouse, so it is possible to learn about the behavior of hundreds of millions of people over many years of interacting with the eBay site around the world. There are thousands of PhDs waiting to be mined from the information in eBay's data warehouse, but sadly for most PhD candidates, eBay is reluctant to share, mostly due to privacy and competitive concerns. In fact, eBay is not unique in its repository of data; companies such as Amazon, Google, and Facebook have an unimaginable magnitude of information stored in their data warehouses, and they also rely on that data to make strategic decisions.

eBay honed its data to get a clearer picture of its RoR. Instead of relying on surveys to determine self-reported satisfaction, which was highly subjective, it could query the database to determine exactly how each user's behavior changed after they had a particular experience on the site. In many respects, the data warehouse had a better understanding of the user's satisfaction than the users themselves. A customer might say on a survey that a particular experience soured them on the site and they decreased their usage afterward, but the information in the data warehouse told the true story.

Designing the Experiment

Working with the data analytics team, eBay came up with an approach it thought could best get at the heart of eBay's true RoR. By examining a very large sample of users in its data warehouse, many hundreds of thousands of individual accounts, it could structure a backward-looking A/B test between two separate pools of accounts to tease out the specific impact of going through the online dispute resolution flows available on the site. eBay decided to focus on active buyer accounts in a particular month. It then analyzed the activity of each account three months prior to the month in question and three months after the month in question:

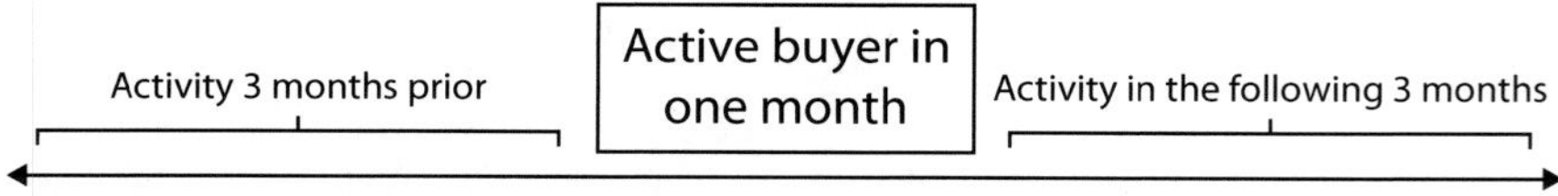

eBay then split that set of accounts into two separate populations: one pool of users who filed a dispute in the active month in question, and another pool of users who did not file a dispute in that month:

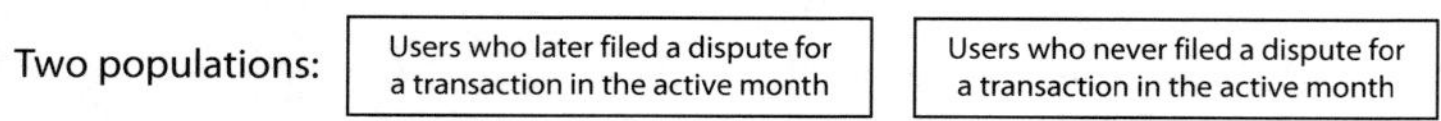

Next, it could generate an Activity Ratio for each account, indicating how active each buyer was on the site for the test periods. This ratio would be calculated by dividing the buyer's Total Payments Volume for the three months post by the buyer's Total Payments Volumes in the three months prior:

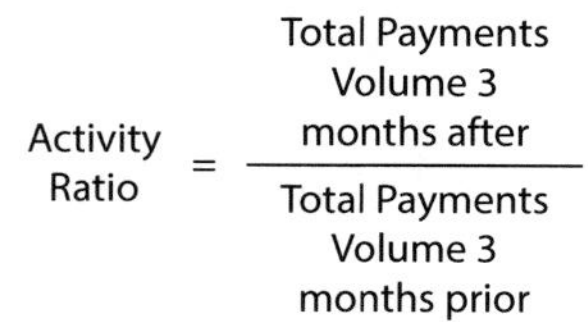

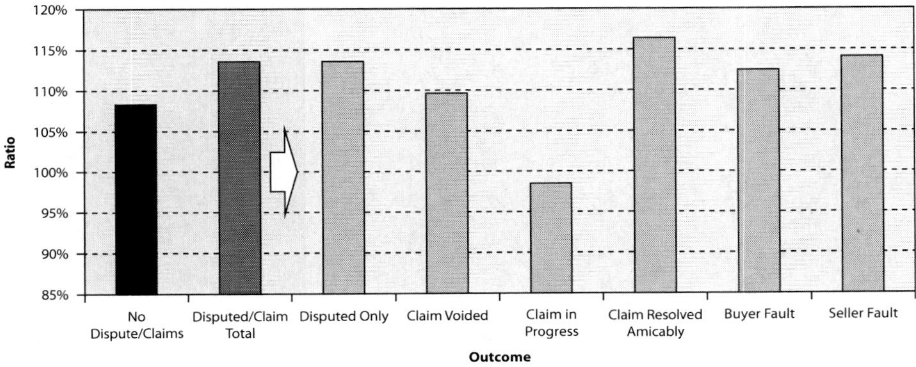

Figure 3.1 Activity Ratios of Buyer Accounts by Outcome Achieved

The beauty of this metric was that it represented the actual impact of going through the online dispute resolution process on the user's behavior, not the buyer's perception of how going through the process impacted their behavior. The other positive aspect of this metric was that it was easily convertible into actual economic benefit to the company because Total Payment Volume can be converted into estimated profits. eBay could determine the exact percentage of profit for every additional dollar of Total Payment Volume processed, so this made the cost-benefit calculation much simpler.

The data spoke, showing a clear benefit to user activity as a result of going through the online dispute resolution process. The results also demonstrated that, on average, users who reported a transaction problem and went through the online dispute resolution process increased their activity on eBay, regardless of outcome. Therefore, buyers who "won" their case increased their activity, but buyers who "lost" their case also increased their activity. Now, it is true that the buyers who lost their case did increase their activity at a slower rate than the buyers who won their cases. Nonetheless, it is notable that, on average, all these types of buyers increased their activity more than buyers who never filed a dispute in the first place.

As you can see in Figure 3.1, the Activity Ratio for buyers who did not file a dispute in the active month was about 108 percent, and the Activity Ratio for buyers who did file a dispute in the active month was about 114 percent. However, more interesting is the fact that every outcome of the dispute process had a higher Activity Ratio than the nonfiling buyers, even when the claim was voided or the buyer was found to be at fault. The group of buyers who had the highest postdispute Activity Ratio was the group of those buyers who had their claims resolved amicably, through mutual agreement with their sellers. This group had an Activity Ratio of approximately 117 percent, higher even than the buyers who won their claims outright (114 percent).

The only group of buyers who filed a dispute and decreased their activity on the site in the three months after the active month were buyers for whom the resolution

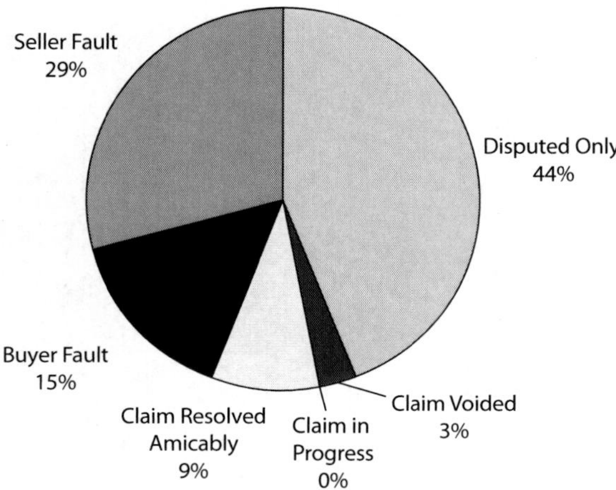

Figure 3.2 Account Distribution of Outcome

process took a very long time (identified as "Claim in Progress" in Figure 3.1). These buyers filed a dispute and, for one reason or another, had the resolution of that dispute take longer than six weeks. If the dispute was resolved within six weeks, then the Activity Ratio was higher than the non-dispute-filing accounts, but if the resolution process stretched beyond six weeks, then the Activity Ratio fell lower than the non-filing accounts. However, as you can see in Figure 3.2, that group of buyer accounts was less than 1 percent of the overall pool of accounts observed.

Another interesting result was that these benefits held for filing buyer accounts across all activity levels, and that these benefits are statistically significant. In Figure 3.3,

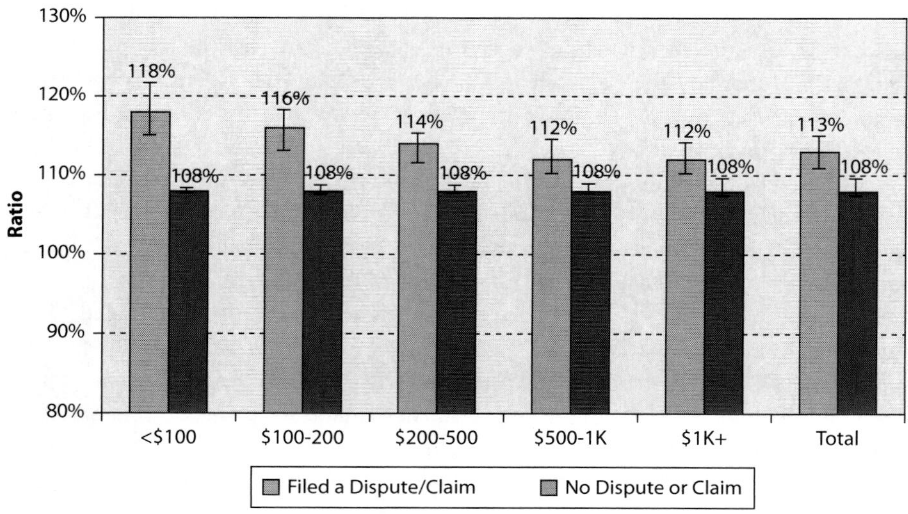

Figure 3.3 Account Distribution of Outcome

you can see that the accounts that filed a dispute had a higher Activity Ratio regardless of whether the buyer spent $100 per month or more than $1,000 per month. The error bars indicate the upper and lower bound of the ratio at the 95 percent confidence level.

Explaining the Results

These conclusions were quite revolutionary. They contradicted several long-held beliefs within the company. Some executives were incredulous when they first reviewed the results, sarcastically suggesting that maybe eBay should intentionally give all buyers a dispute in their first year on the site so as to push up their activity.

However, upon reflection, these results make a lot of sense. It is well understood that user trust is a crucial driver to growing consumer loyalty. Problem resolution is a core component of user trust. Many new users may doubt that if they encounter a transaction problem they will be able to get it resolved quickly and effectively. This lack of confidence acts as a brake on their usage of the service in question. This data made clear that once a buyer gained a firsthand understanding of the available resolution options, and when effective systems were available to help them resolve any transaction problems they encountered, that understanding would encourage them to increase their usage of the service over time.

As an example, imagine you were buying gifts for your family and friends over several weeks leading up to the holiday season. As gift ideas come to you, you may end up purchasing items across a variety of different online marketplaces. Initially, you may have little preference as to which marketplace you use for each item. As the packages arrive in the mail, you may even forget which items you purchased from which marketplaces. As the recipients open their gifts, all you know is that you bought the items online and they arrived without a problem. Buyers often have high expectations for their online purchases, so when everything goes smoothly, the transaction often leaves little to no impression on the purchaser.

However, imagine that one of the items arrives and there is a problem. Maybe it was damaged in shipping, or maybe the wrong item was delivered. When that happens, you as the purchaser must pay individual attention to that particular transaction. You go back to your e-mail, search for the item receipt, and determine where you made the purchase. You then go to the website of the marketplace and try to determine what you need to do to get the problem resolved. That is the moment when a buyer will establish feelings of loyalty or frustration. If the marketplace provides an easy-to-find process for resolving the problem, a strong positive impression is made in the mind of the buyer. If the marketplace does not provide any easy-to-discover process for resolving the problem, the buyer's experience is one of frustration. This creates a strong negative impression.

The results of this research demonstrate that once a buyer goes through an easy-to-navigate ODR process, the buyer establishes a durable connection and affinity for the site in question. The buyer also invests time in learning how to resolve issues on that particular site, and he or she may want to benefit from that understanding in future transactions. Experiencing fast and fair resolutions drives buyers to increase their use of the overall website by a statistically significant amount.

Notably, it is not merely a matter of "winning" a refund. Instead, eBay's data showed that the group of buyers who increased their activity on the site the most were those who filed a dispute and reached an amicable resolution, regardless of the actual amount recovered. The Activity Ratio of these buyers showed the greatest increase, even greater than those users who "won" their case and received a full refund as mandated by the marketplace administrator. This indicated that trust in your fellow users to do the right thing in good faith is more powerful than the belief that a marketplace administrator will intervene and use their power to decide disputes between users who disagree. Having a transaction partner hear your complaint and cooperate in resolving the dispute built more trust than relying on a site administrator to mete out justice in each case. As with the sharing economy, consumers value collaboration—be it in buying/selling or resolving disputes.

As noted, the only buyers who decreased their activity after filing their first dispute were buyers for whom the process took a long time. The frustration associated with a long resolution process outweighed the benefit from getting a positive outcome because buyers value their time more than the money in question when it comes to low-dollar-value transactions. The buyers in these cases learn a different lesson: The marketplace does not have a quick and effective resolution process in place, and that realization displaces any loyalty benefit that comes from educating buyers about the existence of ODR.

External Scrutiny and the Signaling Benefit

Many businesses jealously guard their independence. They feel that external scrutiny will increase costs and reduce their freedom to run their businesses the way they see fit. The cliché is that businesses and Chambers of Commerce want regulators to leave them alone. The consummate entrepreneur wants to make his or her own decisions with an aim to ensure success. However, in this new online commercial environment where trust is the most precious commodity, the ability to conduct business free from external scrutiny is not wholly possible. Transparency is necessary for developing trust. Thus, an online business cannot simply hide resolutions on an obscure help page somewhere and presume that consumers will still feel the site is trustworthy.

If the Internet is knocking down barriers and improving access to information, it stands to reason that the businesses that embrace transparency are best positioned to succeed. Some may speculate that businesses will be reluctant to opt into any system that promises to hold them accountable for the representations they make to consumers. Much like in the offline world, where businesses are subject to decisions by the courts or to scrutiny from regulators, there are concrete economic benefits that accrue to businesses that voluntarily hold themselves accountable and opt into trusted online resolution processes.

As the eBay experience demonstrates, the signaling benefit of opting into a respected and secure resolutions process far outweighs the loss of strategic freedom that comes from a lack of oversight. Consumers are savvy enough to know that businesses who avoid being held accountable are more likely to be difficult to deal with should a problem emerge later in the transaction. It is not hard to envision a future for global commerce where consumers will only purchase from companies that have opted into well-established and respected resolution processes. Consumers will utilize their switching power to avoid merchants that make choices that prevent them from being held accountable.

As a result, the economic benefits of this signaling will be easily demonstrable. Once the business case and RoR is immediately apparent, businesses will be eager to sign up because they will understand that participation in a trust-building mechanism is a powerful differentiator over their competitors. Moreover, it is far better for companies in terms of social, marketing, and economic costs to voluntarily participate in an ODR process than to endure enforcement actions, class actions, and multiple lawsuits.

Takeaways

It is wrong to assume that businesses will always avoid opting into resolution processes because businesses want to make it *more difficult*, not easier, for consumers to get remedies. Instead, businesses will come to understand that providing resolutions leads to loyalty, and ultimately higher profits. Businesspeople want to grow their companies by delivering value and generating profit, and if it can be clearly demonstrated that offering a fast and fair resolutions process will help them achieve that objective, businesspeople will not hesitate to join in.

It is roughly five times harder to attract new customers than to retain current ones, which translates into 25 to 85 percent higher profits merely by retaining 5 percent more current customers. Furthermore, users who achieve a fast and fair resolution become especially loyal customers. Meanwhile, users who do not get a timely solution are much more prone to share their negative experiences on social media and complaint sites. The data analysis at eBay makes a clear and strong case, but similar analyses of the data at sites such as Amazon and Alibaba would likely reinforce the same conclusion.

The good news is that what consumers want is increasingly in line with what improves efficiency and profitability for businesses. Helping businesses understand their RoR will make clear that participation in a global resolutions system is a no-brainer. Not every business will opt in to a fast and fair resolutions process, but the ones that do will grow their market share and succeed over the long term.

CHAPTER 5

Bringing Consumer Advocacy Online

There are many public and nonprofit organizations around the world dedicated to protecting consumers. But just as companies are finding that old ways of offering customer service are out of step with the expectations of consumers, consumer advocates and consumer bureaus are also finding that their own protection tools are similarly out of date. Online dispute resolution can enable consumer protection authorities to stay relevant in the e-commerce era, while increasing their effectiveness and reach.

Challenges Faced by Consumer Advocacy Organizations

Life used to be simpler for consumer advocates. In the days of the old handshake, essentially all of the purchasing activity of a consumer happened within a predefined geographic area. The businesses all had a storefront or a specific postal address. If the consumer had a problem, they could drive down to the store and take it up with the complaints department. If they could not resolve the issue right there, the consumer could write a letter, make a phone call, or come by the office of the consumer advocate in person. Then, the consumer advocate could contact the merchant to try to work out the issue. Everything happened under the umbrella of the consumer advocate's jurisdictional authority.

Now, the situation is much more confused. The Internet has completely changed the game. Consumer protection must navigate a patchwork quilt of different organizations around the world. It is nearly impossible to determine what agency or department takes care of what issues when matters now cross borders so easily. In the United States alone, there are many overlapping agencies and organizations. Students in consumer law classes are often stymied by the myriad of departments and agencies that deal with consumer issues in the United States and how often issues fall through the jurisdictional cracks.

Imagine that you're the head of the National Consumer Protection Bureau in New Zealand. It used to be that 95 percent of the cases brought to your attention were between consumers and businesses in New Zealand. Now, consumers are coming to your office to complain about purchases they have made from businesses in the United States, China, Australia, Europe, and Latin America. Sometimes all they have is a website, and the business is no longer responding to the consumer's e-mails.

As the Head of the Bureau, you have pretty good enforcement power over businesses in New Zealand. If there is a merchant that has become truly problematic, you can bring an action against him in court or perhaps levy fines to incentivize him to clean up his act. But what leverage does New Zealand have over a business in Buenos Aires or Shanghai? International businesses do not care about a warning from the New Zealand Consumer Protection Bureau. They know they can ignore any supposed fines or sanctions because they are not within your jurisdiction.

Let's say that you have created case files for cross-border issues, but you do not know where to send them. If you are especially motivated due the audacity of the consumer grievance, you may go above and beyond to send letters to the Embassies of other countries located in New Zealand. You may even have the resources to send letters to the New Zealand Embassies located around the world. That would really be going the extra mile. However, in all honesty, your staff would probably not have the time to invest in such outreach. Most likely, such efforts would be futile. Diplomatic staffs are thin enough, and this type of thing is generally outside of their expertise, not to mention their jurisdiction.

Even worse, the laws are different all over the world. New Zealand protects consumers pretty aggressively, but many other countries do not have similar protections. Your small staff cannot be expected to know the consumer protection regulations in 50 different countries, not to mention all the language and cultural challenges. Good luck even locating and translating the applicable law! Even the savviest consumer law professors struggle to track down international consumer protection laws.

So what is the consumer advocate to do? If she does gather enough gumption to assist a consumer with a cross-border purchase, she has to find some way to communicate with the merchant, a local consumer advocate, or the judicial system in that country. Of course, these entities may ignore her attempts. They have their own local consumer issues to worry about. Moreover, not all nations have such consumer protection entities, or the entities they have may be largely ineffective.

As an advocate, you feel for the consumers, who are even more desperate than you are. When they come in the door to speak to you, you can see the resignation in their eyes. They do not have good resolution options for dealing with these cross-border issues, and they know that you do not have many more options than they have. It is no surprise that an extremely small percentage of aggrieved consumers even tell you about these cross-border issues.

Your best bet may be consumer education. You can advise consumers not to shop outside of New Zealand or coach them on how to avoid problems. However, the convenience, wide selection, and price advantages available on the Internet mean the trend of international purchasing is not going to slow down any time soon. On your bad days, you wonder if the expansion of e-commerce means that consumer advocacy organizations like yours have no power to assist with cross-border purchases. Nonetheless, you realize that strong and effective consumer advocacy is even more vital than it has been in the past. However, just like every industry and service that has been disrupted by technology, consumer advocates have to fundamentally change the way they work in order to stay relevant to the times. Commerce is being completely changed by technology. Consumer advocates need to evolve their strategies in a similarly dramatic way.

It is also important to note that consumer agencies throughout the world have already sought to expand consumer education. However, education is not enough. Even the savviest consumers get stuck with poor purchases. One can research a product to death and still get a lemon. A consumer law professor may do diligent research, review all contract terms, and believe she has made a financially and legally wise purchase but still experience a mountain of problems. Furthermore, she likely will not have the time or money to pursue claims regarding the purchase problems, especially for small-dollar purchases. Like most consumers, even supposed experts usually "lump it" and forgo deserved remedies. Indeed, consumers of all walks of life crave low-cost or free ODR processes to promote real consumer protection.

Addressing the Dearth of Information

We all know that there are billions of e-commerce transactions taking place all over the world, but consumer protection authorities have almost zero visibility into these transactions. Approximately 1 to 3 percent of global e-commerce transactions are generating disputes, but most consumer advocates never learn about them. If anything, authorities may gather some information from online complaints via a reporting form on the consumer authority's website. But the inconvenience of that channel, combined with skepticism about what consumer advocates can really do to help get a situation resolved, artificially constrain these reports. Again, most consumers simply will not go through the unwieldy and seemingly futile process of filling out the complaint form on a consumer advocate website unless they know that such an action will generate results.

At the same time, merchants and marketplaces are reluctant to share data with consumer protection authorities because they fear that regulators will misinterpret data out of context or use it against them in some punitive way. This leads to an information asymmetry between businesses and the consumer protection authorities. Why would a merchant share data with authorities that could generate enforcement actions against him?

In sum, this leaves consumer protection authorities flying blind. They must rely on very limited data, and that limited data may lead to inaccurate conclusions about the full spectrum of issues being experienced by consumers. For example, a merchant selling a remote-controlled helium-inflated flying shark may suddenly be on the authorities' radar as a "bad actor" after the proactive, squeaky-wheel consumers file complaints alleging that the remote control does not work. The authorities could then get on the case and waste resources in pursuit of this merchant.

Greater data, however, would have revealed that the remote requires 24 hours of charging before it will work. Unfortunately, this information was accidentally left out of the product documentation. Routine data sharing would have prevented this waste by allowing authorities to immediately notify complainers of the need to charge the remote. At the same time, the merchant could issue clarified instructions. However, merchants often fail to report such snafus to authorities for (perhaps shortsighted) fear that sharing this mistake with authorities could lead to deceptive trade practices claims.

What consumer advocates need is a new platform that can help them get real-time visibility into a much greater percentage of the consumer issues experienced within their geography. There also needs to be a simple, streamlined way for consumer advocates to a) easily and automatically receive reports from consumers, b) communicate with merchants to get the full picture, and c) track each case to closure in a short window of time. Consumer protection authorities need to have a much clearer understanding of the day-to-day realities within their jurisdictions.

Furthermore, a friendlier process would encourage self-reporting and open lines of communication to ease displaced fears of consumer protection enforcement. Indeed, governments around the world continue to encourage self-reporting as means for increasing transparency around consumer protection issues and providing safe harbors for the "good kids" who do fess up and address mistakes.

This data visibility can also help consumer protection authorities identify breakout situations with individual merchants, which may inspire rapid responses to minimize the number of victimized consumers. Real-time data translates into real-time remedies. Imagine transparency that leads to a map of the consumer protection authority's area with new reports highlighted per product category. This type of functionality could be quite robust. The map could show the incidents by severity, frequency, and outcome. This kind of real-time data visualization can both significantly improve the understanding of the consumer protection authority as to what is really going on in its target geography, and enable rapid action when appropriate.

International Cooperation

Technology enables much more efficient cooperation among consumer advocates across geographies. The New Zealand Consumer Protection Bureau has cultural context and ready access to consumers and merchants within New Zealand. The Hong Kong Office of the Consumer Advocate has ready access to consumers and merchants in Hong Kong. If a consumer comes into the New Zealand office with a complaint about a merchant in Hong Kong, technology can enable the easy notification from New Zealand to Hong Kong, so that the Hong Kong Office of the Consumer Advocate can investigate the matter. Vice versa, if a consumer comes into the Hong Kong office to complain about a New Zealand seller, the exchange can work the other way. If cases can be captured in a common data format using compatible case management systems, then robust cooperation is not difficult to achieve.

Efforts like the UNCITRAL ODR Working Group have envisioned these types of reciprocal jurisdiction arrangements for years. However, the technology was not yet mature enough to deliver on the vision. Now, with the EU ODR regulation coming into force, and with ODR platforms reaching higher levels of scalability and flexibility, the vision can finally be realized. Consumer protection authorities can opt into global protocols for case and data exchange to enable seamless cooperation across jurisdictions. This means that each consumer will have an entry point into the global redress process in their native language, appropriate to their local culture and regulatory environment, but with global reach.

Tripwires and Mass Claims

A common criticism of face-to-face dispute resolution is that it personalizes every dispute. Because matters are traditionally kept confidential, consumers are not aware of cases filed by other consumers that fit the same fact pattern. The onus is always on individual consumers to report their issue, and to pursue it all the way through to resolution. But there may be issues where hundreds or thousands of consumers were victimized by the same problem—and it would be unreasonable to expect every single one of those victims to individually file a case in order to get redress.

For example, consider a mobile telephone company that accidentally charged the wrong amount for international text messages for a three-week period. It was supposed to be 1 cent per text message, but it actually was entered into the billing system as 5 cents per text message. Users who expected to get a bill for $10 ended up with a bill for $50. More than 45,000 users were subscribed to the plan in question, and unsurprisingly, the disputes rolled in after the bills were sent out.

However, not every user will be aware of the overcharge. Maybe only 30 percent of the telephone plan subscribers noticed the dispute, and only about 20 percent (around 8,500 customers) actually reported it and requested a refund. Is it fair or reasonable to only pay out to the 8,500 customers who reported the problem? An economist could argue that it is fair and rational to pay only those who complain because (1) only the complainers were actually harmed in the sense that they felt it was worth their resources to pursue the claim and (2) all consumers benefit when the company is able to pass on cost savings (or extra profit) through lower prices. However, the better answer is to say *no*, it is not fair to grease only the squeaky wheels. The better approach is to acknowledge the error and proactively refund all of the customers who were victimized by it. This is especially true if you want to avoid the costs and hassles of class or enforcement actions.

Technology can make this kind of mass claims resolution much more efficient and effective, while preventing the publicity and additional costs and complexities of class actions. One way to implement effective mass claims in ODR is through the use of a tripwire. If many complaints against a single merchant fit the same pattern (say, 100 users reporting that they were overcharged in the same fashion), the onus can then shift back onto the merchant so that the merchant must do an investigation as to how many consumers may have been victimized by the issue in question.

Tripwires also can facilitate cooperation between private/nonprofit consumer advocates and public consumer protection authorities. For example, individual cases might not make it onto the radar of a regulator, but if more than 1,000 cases with the same fact pattern are filed in the system against the same merchant, the system could automatically alert the Federal Trade Commission (FTC) to notify them about the situation. Such an automatic escalation would alert the public of the danger that may otherwise remain private, and it would help address current complaints regarding the privatization of statutory and other public policy claims through traditional arbitration and class waivers.

These tripwires are a smart way for consumer advocacy organizations to provide mass redress in situations where many consumers may have suffered from the same issue. The class action process is intended to provide this kind of mass redress; however, as we have described, it is often subject to abuse. Combined with real-time data visibility, tripwire mechanisms can enable consumer protection authorities to identify patterns of consumer problems and immediatly reach out to the merchants in question to address the problem. Merchants can also use their participation in mass claim resolutions to help protect themselves against later class action exposure, which can be far more damaging and expensive.

Confidentiality and Privacy

Consumer advocacy organizations are also very sensitive to data security. Online consumers frequently have their personal information shared without their knowledge or consent. These privacy violations can lead to issues for consumers down the line, as they receive marketing information that they do not want, suffer from increased risk of identity theft, or face financial or employment disadvantages due to the private information that was shared without their knowledge. By having data about consumer complaints, consumer protection authorities can design a system that better protects the confidentiality and security of consumers, helping to ensure that privacy breaches are caught before they get out of control.

Privacy violations are very difficult to monitor. Often, consumers are unaware that their information is being shared without their consent; only after a consumer starts to see the impact of the breach is it clear that something has gone wrong. Trying to resolve a privacy violation is kind of like trying to unring a bell: Once the information is shared, it cannot be "unshared." The key issue is to identify the problem as quickly as possible to prevent it from getting worse. It is also very unclear what types of redress are appropriate in a privacy violation scenario. There is not a clear dollar value or reimbursement amount for an affected consumer when a privacy violation occurs.

There are longstanding ODR systems for reporting privacy violations, such as TRUSTe's Privacy Watchdog Dispute Resolution. However, the existing systems are not well integrated into transaction environments. This makes it difficult for consumers to be aware of these protections. In turn, they do not take advantage of the systems or obtain remedies. Additionally, this dearth of information capture again contributes to the lack of enforcement by consumer protection authorities. They cannot address issues that they do not know about.

It should also go without saying that any consumer resolution system must itself abide by best practices in data security and data protection. If consumers are reporting their concerns into a global resolution system, they must have full disclosure around who will see the information they are submitting. It may be appropriate for aggregated and anonymized trend data to be shared with consumer advocates, but not for specific information about individual disputes or personally identifiable information to be shared. The systems design must abide by the most stringent data protection rules in the world so as to ensure it will always be in compliance in every jurisdiction.

Ease of Access

One of the top takeaways from the *New Handshake* is that consumers crave easy and user-friendly remedy systems. Consumers are sick of the runaround of the old call-in customer service and the subjective unfairness that occurs when remedies are doled out to only the most lucrative clientele. It is annoying and unfair to get a raw deal due to your income or education. Moreover, it is frustrating to invest time in filing complaints with consumer protection authorities that go unanswered.

Nonetheless, one of the biggest challenges consumer protection and consumer advocacy organizations have is getting access to consumer issues at the earliest possible stage and having the bandwidth to address complaints that are filed. For example, a consumer protection nonprofit in a particular geography that has a complaint filing form on its home page is unlikely to attract a consumer's attention, and a consumer is unlikely to be sufficiently proactive to find the site and fill out the form. Most consumers simply lack the time and resources for such a process that is housed away from the point-of-sale. If a transaction has taken place in another environment somewhere else on the Internet, only the most motivated consumers will pursue the case so aggressively that they will search out the website of an unrelated consumer protection advocacy organization and then re-report all the details of the transaction in question. This is especially true when the consumer (often correctly) assumes that he will never get a response.

Instead, a functional system should integrate the process for reporting buyer issues into every transaction environment. If the initiation button for reporting a complaint is on the home page of the merchant's website, it is very easy for the consumer to click that button, fill out a couple of questions detailing the claim, and then see the case all the way through to the end via one portal. This should also be integrated directly into that consumer's account page within the merchant site so that the consumer could see all of the items that he has purchased within his account and report an issue with a single click next to the item in question. The consumer should only have to file the complaint once in order to get a remedy.

Online dispute resolution technology makes this kind of embeddable resolution process very easy to implement. This, in turn, makes reporting and redress much easier for consumers while augmenting information available to consumer advocates and organizations. By offering one-stop shopping for resolutions, consumer protection organizations would become especially relevant and effective. They would make remedy systems real by empowering their constituent consumers to file complaints once at the point-of-sale site. There would be no need for surfing the web to find the appropriate venue for their claim.

Lack of Resources

Another challenge facing consumer advocates is the lack of resources. Consumer protection groups are often chronically underresourced, which continually puts them at a disadvantage when they are advocating for consumers. Technology can enable operation of resolution systems at a scale that enables the generation of resources that can better support the activities of consumer protection authorities and consumer advocacy organizations. As noted above, consumer protection authorities simply lack the resources to deal with consumer complaints. However, use of ODR can address this.

Much like an insurance model, each individual complaint above a certain specified volume can generate a very modest fee from the merchant. This small fee provides a modest disincentive for the merchant that may make the merchant more eager to proactively resolve issues before they become formal complaints. Over time, the fees generated may create a pool of resources that can be used to compensate consumers who have had negative experiences with particular merchants but for whom a reimbursement from the merchant is not a possibility. These resources can also assist consumer protection authorities and consumer advocacy organizations in marketing the availability of these redress tools. It also allows them to further develop their platforms so that they are more discoverable, easy to use, and effective.

Merchants may also want to add more functionality to their resolution systems for internal purposes. Perhaps they want to upgrade their reporting or put in a connector to their customer support ticketing system. These kind of technological additions can also generate revenue that feeds back into the development of the overall system.

There is always a risk with generating revenue from merchants to support consumer advocacy. That risk must be taken seriously. If the financial dependence on payments from merchants becomes too great, it can compromise the neutrality of the consumer advocate. However, if these payments are well designed, intermediated by a program administrator, governed by policy instead of solicited by the recipients, and automated, then concerns around the potential bias can be ameliorated. Everyone will benefit from continuous improvement in the technology that will undergird this global resolutions system. Consumer advocates stand to gain the most. Thus, we need to find a way to generate reliable revenue that can fund the continued evolution and improvement of the system.

Providing Human-Powered Redress

While the benefits to consumer advocates come mostly from automated resolution processes, some cases will require the attention from a human neutral mediator or arbitrator to reach resolution. Consumer advocates are the likely organizations to provide these human-powered online redress processes, but always in response to requests from the disputants themselves. Perhaps consumers should be offered a menu of services they can choose from depending on a) the specifics of the case and b) how a seller responds to the initial complaint. This multidoor process may be more satisfactory and productive than unidimensional dispute resolution procedures because it would provide consumers with choices and empower them to pick their preferred path toward a final outcome. The consumers will always be in control of their own journey toward a solution. Indeed, studies confirm that claimants are most satisfied when they have a voice and choice in the dispute resolution process.

Mediation is the logical next step beyond direct communication (mediation is just assisted negotiation), but some cases will likely justify an evaluative outcome if the parties cannot reach a settlement through mutual agreement. This evaluative step will definitely require both sides in the case to voluntarily agree to submit the case to a mutually acceptable arbitrator. Allowing for an evaluative "last stop" in the process helps prevent parties from using delay tactics to waylay resolution. Neither companies nor consumers benefit from time wasting discussions that don't go anywhere, and in some cases they may not take nonbinding processes seriously if the process will not end the dispute.

Commitment to any ODR process must be voluntary and properly regulated to ensure fairness and foster open-minded use of the process. Online mediation and arbitration services provided through this system must instead be balanced, fair, and efficient. The ODR field has a lot of experience in building human-powered online resolution systems that meet these criteria. The process must be user-friendly, with guidance for consumers on how to structure complaints and upload information supporting their claims. Forms and wizards should largely ease or eliminate the need for legal assistance required for pursuing complaints. The online system must also be geared for consumers of all education levels.

Moreover, it is essential that the online mediators and arbitrators who serve as neutrals in the ODR processes be truly neutral and properly trained. ODR rules should require that human neutrals go through training and obtain a certification.

Perhaps the certification and monitoring process can be overseen by a public regulator, such as the Consumer Financial Protection Bureau in the United States. The rules also should provide for a mechanism to gather user feedback on neutral performance in order to foster continual system improvements and to ensure a continued high quality of service.

Takeaways

Technology is transforming the work of consumer advocates as much as it has transformed commerce itself. Evolving needs and expectations of consumers will unquestionably change the work of consumer advocacy organizations. What consumer advocates lack is an updated set of tools and processes that give them the visibility and connection required to protect consumers in our newly networked age. Once those tools are in place, the role of consumer advocates will be more important and relevant than ever before.

It is not enough to provide process without providing enforceable outcomes. Consumer advocates must have the wherewithal to deliver resolutions and decisions that they can make stick. Cross-jurisdictional cooperation, certification, and monitoring can help to ensure enforcement power. An ODR process is only as good as its ability to enforce the outcomes it delivers. These tools and processes will go a long way toward giving consumer advocacy organizations what they need to ensure adherence to resolutions delivered by the system.

ODR promises to ease many of the cost, time, and bias challenges that have hindered consumer advocates from extending their services across the Internet. These tools will help consumer advocates revive companies' commitments to consumers by holding companies accountable and reinforcing consumer trust.

CHAPTER

6 Ethical Considerations

The introduction of technology into consumer resolution processes raises some challenging new ethical issues, not only for parties and neutrals, but also for ODR systems designers. While there has been growing interest in ethical standards for face-to-face ADR practice over the past few decades, there has been little to no attention to the new and different concerns raised for ODR practitioners and designers. It is therefore vital to consider ethical standards for any proposed ODR redress system if it is to have a chance to survive and succeed.

When ODR first emerged in the late 1990s, most systems designers presumed that the best approach was to simply replicate offline dispute mechanisms online. These mechanisms had been refined over decades of practice, so the assumption was that they represented best practices for helping parties find solutions. Most of the earliest ODR systems simply took the well-established approaches of face-to-face dispute resolution processes and duplicated them in code.

That approach was short-sighted. ODR systems designers discovered relatively quickly that "same old" did not translate well online. The Internet opened new frontiers for resolving disputes through means that would never work face to face. As a corollary, there were things parties and neutrals had always done in face-to-face dispute resolution that were impractical, if not impossible, online.

This is true as well with ethical guidelines. The alternative dispute resolution (ADR) field has worked hard to create effective ethical guidelines for dispute resolution practice since the 1970s. Courses in ADR ethics are taught at many law schools, and there are excellent articles, books, and working groups focusing on the topic. However, the ethical dilemmas facing ODR practitioners are quite different than those facing offline practitioners. Technology raises complex ethical quandaries that have not been adequately addressed in existing training materials and standards.

For example, the ability to record all negotiation communications can raise concerns about confidentiality and privacy. The ability to instantly access all sorts of information in the midst of a negotiation may lead to the introduction of data that can bias or derail an otherwise promising agreement. Parties may not be able to resist the temptation to secretly loop third parties into online communications or to Google the background of their counterparts to learn about unrelated but compromising events in their past. Although these actions may appear patently improper, the standards are not sufficiently clear to encompass all the perils and possibilities of the ODR systems. It is therefore clear that new guidelines are required for the online world.

Most existing ethical guidelines focus on in-person mediators and arbitrators. The American Arbitration Association (AAA)/Society of Professionals in Dispute Resolution (SPIDR)/American Bar Association (ABA) Ethical Standards address concerns like self-determination, impartiality, and conflicts of interest. The standards are written for human facilitators, with the goal of providing a fair and transparent process to the disputants in each individual case. Nonetheless, even these supposedly clear standards are murky in many cases. The Internet is already raising questions for ADR practitioners in face-to-face processes (i.e., deciding whether a party "friending" an arbitrator on Facebook crosses ethical lines, even if the party has 500 "friends").

These questions raised by technology are amplified in ODR. For example, many of the facilitation tasks are handled by software in ODR. Computer code can be more objective and neutral. It is generally unaffected by some of the behavioral and psychological factors that create challenges for in-person dispute resolvers. It is also uninhibited by some practicalities of face-to-face processes. For example, software code will not rewrite itself in order to finish up early to catch a plane, or push the parties into a less-than-perfect solution in order to make a higher contingency fee.

Although we do have to be concerned about the ethical standards of the neutrals (e.g., mediators and arbitrators) in ODR systems, we also need to consider the ethical dilemmas confronted by the system designers before the first case is filed. Indeed, humans do create the code—and it is that creation that must be in compliance with ethical norms and standards.

Online Ethical Dilemmas for Neutrals

A 2010 article, "Virtual Virtues: Ethical Considerations for an Online Dispute Resolution (ODR) Practice," laid out some of the ethical dilemmas facing mediators and arbitrators interacting online. The main areas of focus identified were impartiality, cost, and confidentiality. A more recent article by Dan Rainey, "Third Party Ethics in the Age of the Fourth Party," identified three primary areas of focus: confidentiality/privacy, access to the process, and competence. Let's combine the two lists and examine each of these broad categories in turn.

Impartiality and Competence

Any dispute resolution practitioner knows that impartiality is key. It is what parties most desire—and a reputation for impartiality is essential to a practitioner's success. Those in the field nonetheless know that true neutrality is impossible.

Practitioners are human, after all. We all come to any situation with the baggage of our behavioral, social, and psychological propensities. For example, dispute resolvers have an obligation to assist parties in feeling comfortable during facilitative discussions. That often means that the resolver should try to address power differentials. However, a mediator who aids a "weaker" party in an attempt to increase process fairness is no longer neutral. Furthermore, mediators usually harbor implicit biases that inevitably impact their party interactions.

In an online context, mediators bear many of the same ethical obligations they carry in the face-to-face world. However, they must apply and interpret those obligations in an expanded fashion online. For example, online mediators must of course strive to be impartial, and must recuse themselves if they feel that they cannot act impartially in a given case. Furthermore, as is true for face-to-face mediators, the temptation exists to learn more about the background of the parties in a particular case. However, the temptation is stronger in ODR because one is not sitting in front of the parties. What is to stop a mediator from opening a new browser during online discussions to do a Google search? Mediators online and offline must understand their ethical obligations and stand strong to resist such ethical lapses. If a mediator conducts a background search and discovers something that may make it difficult to treat the parties impartially, he or she needs to understand the ethical obligation to step down.

All mediators also have the obligation to be competent in the assistance they provide to negotiating parties. This obligation may be slightly different for online mediators, however, in that they must have competence in creating comfort through online environments. An online mediator must understand the ODR process and ably explain the ground rules, as well as how computer-mediated communications may impact a process. The mediator must be aware of parties' technological aptitude: If one party is very comfortable with technology, types 100 words a minute, and is online at every hour of the day, whereas the other party is more hesitant about technology, has difficulty typing, and can only access the Internet once every other day over a slow connection in a public library, then the mediator has an ethical obligation to compensate for that differential in designing the process. That may mean in some cases that the mediator may have an ethical obligation to move negotiations offline in order to ensure a level playing field for both participants. This expanded conceptualization of competence may have to address questions of technology access and venue in ODR, while the face-to-face conceptualization of competence may focus more narrowly on the mediator's behavior in the room with the parties.

Cost and Accessibility

Cost and accessibility are also core considerations. Can the disputants effectively participate in the negotiation process? Is the process easy for them to navigate? Once they begin the process, do they understand how it will work?

More fundamentally, can the parties afford the process? Is it free or extremely low cost? Does the cost outweigh any potential recovery?

ODR processes may be easy to initiate at the outset, as they may require only a few clicks to file a claim. However, an ODR process may be difficult to navigate after process inception. Online arbitrators and mediators therefore have an obligation to fully educate negotiating parties on their obligations as participants upfront including all possible costs they may need to bear.

Mediators also must be forthright about how they will be compensated for their time. Obviously, they must avoid any compensation that is conditional on a particular outcome to a dispute. However, they also should disclose who is paying for a process to avoid any appearance of bias. Impressions of bias mean everything when it comes to party perception. If the services of an online mediator are being covered by an organization that has a particular interest in the outcome of the mediation, that potential conflict must be disclosed to the parties. Moreover, it goes without saying that mediators must never impose procedural obligations or costs on a party in an effort to frustrate them, or to encourage them to settle. Both online and offline practitioners should know better.

Confidentiality and Privacy

As noted earlier, parties are very concerned with privacy. Indeed, if you ask users to name their number one concern about using ODR, odds are they will say privacy and confidentiality. In face-to-face mediations, it is common for mediators to assure the parties of the confidentiality of the information shared in the privacy of the negotiation session. If a negotiator or mediator takes notes during the session, she may tear them up and dispose of them in front of the parties to make her commitment to confidentiality clear. Mediators can look parties in the eye and say confidently, "Everything said in this session is confidential."

In contrast, online neutrals are a seeming mystery to the parties. You cannot look the mediator or arbitrator in the eye or see her "tear up the notes" to assure the parties a conversation will remain confidential. Some parties may therefore be very concerned that the information they share in the process will be archived on a server somewhere and may eventually become public. Parties may worry that the information may emerge later through some unpredictable channel, perhaps turning up in a Google search at a future date.

It is therefore essential that ethical obligations around information security are clear for online mediators and arbitrators. Furthermore, systems must be secure and there must be systems in place to ensure confidentiality and privacy of anything submitted in ODR. Nonetheless, what is to stop parties from sharing information gathered in ODR negotiations with others outside of the process? It may therefore be important to have parties digitally agree to the ethical obligation to respect the confidentiality of private communications in a dispute resolution process. A violation may be as easy as forwarding on a confidential e-mail to a friend or colleague, done with a split-second decision and a click of a mouse. This ethical obligation not to do so must therefore be made explicit by agreement at the beginning of each ODR process.

The issue is further complicated because there is a spectrum of confidentiality in online interactions. It is not as simple as information being private or public. Maybe the particular communications within an ODR process are confidential, but the final decision or settlement agreement will be publicly available. Or, maybe data from hundreds (or thousands or millions) of negotiations will be aggregated, and statistics for the full case volume will be released without any personally identifiable information. It is more complicated to disclose limitations on confidentiality in online settings when there are so many possible ways for information to be shared or not shared.

This is further complicated by evolving perceptions of privacy. For example, many of the disputes in the eBay ODR system involved disputants who were eager to shout about their frustrations from the rooftops. The parties in those e-commerce matters were not as concerned about confidentiality as offline disputants might have been. In fact, many of the disputants on eBay presumed that their every message and response was being monitored by administrators and case managers. Sometimes in the middle of a dispute, one of the parties would start talking to a generic eBay administrator who they presumed was listening in. Parties would also be on their best behavior because they presumed eBay was watching, and because they thought they might be penalized for bad behavior if they did not behave themselves. Similarly, people will often joke in e-mail or Skype that the NSA is listening in to all of their posts. These shifting standards make it all the more important to be explicit about privacy and confidentiality at the outset in each online negotiation.

Many neutrals now use freely available online tools like e-mail, Skype, text messages, and calendar invites to interact with their parties. As any information security expert will tell you, these channels are not secure. ADR professionals may say to their parties that they will abide by their ethical standard of confidentiality, protecting the privacy and confidentiality of their negotiation communications. However, to meet that standard, neutrals may in fact have an ethical obligation to only use communication channels that have been designed to support secure information exchange. If ADR practitioners want to live up to the face-to-face ethical obligation of maintaining party confidentiality, they should migrate any online communications into software systems that are specifically designed to protect participant privacy.

Notably, lawyers also neglect to understand the insecurity of many messaging systems. E-mails and texts are not all encrypted and secure. Law students must learn from day one about digital security of client information. Similarly, ODR systems in the *New Handshake* must be created with security in mind. Built-in encryption and security for communications are key attributes and benefits of ODR over old ways of resolving consumer claims.

Ethical Dilemmas for Systems Designers

That is not to say that technology equates ethics in all cases. Indeed, technology raises an even more complex set of ethical dilemmas for systems designers. While individual mediators and arbitrators have a reasonable set of ethical questions to wrestle with, ODR systems designers face an even more complex and confusing range of dilemmas. Suddenly the individual (or team of individuals) programming ODR systems has the ability to exert enormous influence over the resolution process. Furthermore, an ODR software program may participate in a hundred, thousand, or a million processes, thereby impacting an unimaginable number of outcomes.

To some extent, individual neutrals must focus on the specific needs of their parties on a case-by-case basis, but systems designers need to think about broader questions of procedural justice. There has to be some set of standards or best practices for ODR if it is to serve consumers' needs. Standards are necessary to prevent ODR from dying in a chaotic graveyard of kangaroo courts. If ODR systems are to survive and thrive, they have to strive to meet some set of ethical standards.

Accordingly, many working groups over the past 10 to 15 years have examined the appropriate standards for quality ODR service delivery. These groups have come from international standards organizations (e.g., the International Standards Organization, the European Standards Organization), bar associations (e.g., the ABA's Task Force on eCommerce and ODR), legislatures (e.g., the Canadian Working Group on eCommerce and Consumers), and international industry groups (e.g., Internet Corporation for Assigned Names and Numbers [ICANN]). As a result of these extensive efforts, we have a strong idea of the core ethical obligations online dispute resolution (ODR) systems should abide by. As summarized by Jeff Aresty and Ruha Devanesan in their chapter in the book *Online Dispute Resolution: Theory and Practice*, ethical ODR systems need to be transparent, independent, impartial, effective, fair, accessible, flexible, and affordable. Each of these considerations for systems designers will be addressed in turn.

Transparent

Transparency helps to ensure that an ODR system is operating the way that it should. ICANN's Uniform Domain Name Dispute Resolution Protocol (UDRP) is an excellent example of a transparent online dispute resolution process (even though it may have challenges in some of the other ethical standards). Under the UDRP, every case filing and decision is publicly accessible. This has led to quite a bit of external scrutiny for the UDRP process. As one may expect, it is not necessarily comfortable for the participants and the dispute resolution service providers to have full public scrutiny for all cases coming through the system. However, transparency can be a very important way for ODR systems to retain public trust, and for problems to be detected quickly and resolved. Much like how sunlight laws in the public sector promote honesty, process transparency in ODR is key to combating systemic bias.

Independent

Procedural independence is crucial for disputants to trust outcomes delivered through ODR processes. If a resolution system is administered either directly or indirectly by one of the parties to the disputes, it will appear suspect. That is not to say that merchants should never provide ODR processes for resolution of disputes with their customers. Instead, the key is for system designers to establish means for ensuring that the code and system are independent of the merchant and customer service staff.

Furthermore, even if the system is administered externally, independence is not a foregone conclusion. For example, it will appear suspect if there are unequal financial obligations between the parties and the administrator. Again, the ODR systems designers will have to address the operation of the process to ensure that the system is free from influence that might tip the scales one way or another.

Impartial

Impartiality is obviously connected to independence. However, it is slightly different. Impartiality refers to the level playing field of the resolution process. The system should not be tilted in a particular direction. Even if the system is independent of both parties, financially and from an administrative standpoint, the coding and design may favor particular outcomes. That would undermine the impartiality of the system.

That means that the ODR systems must be designed to provide a fair hearing to both sides, without any systemic bias. Decisions must be based entirely on the case facts. Transparency also is essential to prevent any perception that there is a thumb on the scale for any particular position or party. Any such perception will harm, if not destroy, public trust. This means that ODR systems designers and coders also have an ethical obligation to be impartial.

It may seem at first blush that software code is inherently unbiased: It is just a bunch of algorithms and calculations (or some such computer "stuff" above our pay grade). However, coding is subject to the bias of the programmer and systems designer. As Larry Lessig has written, software code governs behavior online in a manner similar to the way the law governs behavior in the offline world. Software designers also have great power because users cannot easily change how it works. Users of online negotiation software programs are like mice running through a maze. They cannot change the path presented to them, so they must simply navigate the options available in an effort to reach their desired conclusion.

For instance, if a programmer really wants two negotiators to settle in a particular case, the programmer can present selective information to one side that urges them to ask for less money. The programmer could simultaneously present information to the other side to urge them to offer more money. That may increase the zone of potential agreement (ZOPA) in the negotiation, which increases the likelihood of settlement. Or, a programmer could gather information from one side while offering assurances that the information will be kept confidential, but in reality the software is sharing that information with admin or case managers who can surreptitiously pass it along to outside parties. The individual mediator or negotiator in these cases might behave ethically, but the software itself (or, more accurately, the designer who built the software) may have introduced components that violate ethical principles. These types of systems design challenges were not contemplated in most of the ethical rules promulgated in the ADR field for face-to-face practice.

Effective

ODR processes must be effective in delivering fast and fair outcomes. If the mechanism provided is ineffective at reaching decisions in a timely manner, it will quickly lose credibility. Slow processes that create a lot of churn with little progress will frustrate parties and urge them to stonewall or drop out. Suspicions may emerge that an intentionally ineffective and inefficient process was put into place to discourage filings. However, speed alone does not equate to effectiveness. The process also must be effective at delivering just outcomes. If the process is quick and efficient, but delivers flawed or wildly inconsistent outcomes, it will be ineffective.

Fair

If a resolution process is transparent and parties can examine its design in advance of any dispute arising and they all agree that its fundamentals are fair then it can be said that the process is procedurally just. Once a dispute arises, that process may deliver an outcome that one party or the other may feel is incorrect, but the system design in and of itself can still be considered fair. This standard of fairness is much more achievable. Much like the court system, we cannot build a resolution process that ensures every user will always get what they want. However, we can design a resolution process that external evaluators deem just in that it will not introduce external considerations that corrupt the outcomes it generates.

Accessible

Some excellent dispute resolution processes are unimpeachably fair and well designed, but they are nearly impossible to access. Likewise, regardless of the online mediators' and arbitrators' credentials, the process is useless if the parties have too much difficulty finding how to file a case because the initiation button is buried in fine print. It must be easy to access the process, regardless of education or resources. Sometimes merchants or marketplaces will create a well-designed resolution process but then hide it, secretly (or not so secretly) hoping that their customers will not notice or use it.

Shortsighted merchants also may not want to encourage their customers to assert their complaints. This approach is unwise and could prove costly. Businesses with a long-view realize that they should welcome valid claims and offer an easily accessible process. That is fair and responsible. Moreover, burying a resolution process takes away any value of the implementation costs and robs the business of the opportunity to learn about problems with their goods and services before they become bigger problems. To meet these ethical standards, ODR systems must be discoverable and accessible, independent of how well designed they are internally.

Affordable

Affordability is related to accessibility. Many dispute resolution processes are well designed, and even may be easy to navigate. However, they are inaccessible if they are too expensive. A process not worth its costs is useless. The judicial process suffers from this ailment in some respects, as individuals who cannot afford quality representation often are forced to either not utilize the system, or self-represent and get bad outcomes. Face-to-face arbitration also has suffered on this count.

ODR processes must balance the value of procedural protections with their costs, so as to offer quality resolutions that disputants can pay for without undue burden. It goes without saying that the best ODR is free to consumers. Ideally, there should be means for funding a resolution process that preserves independence and impartiality without requiring payment from participants. Alternatively, the systems should be very low cost for consumers. If they are too expensive, they are violating this ethical obligation.

Flexible

ODR processes must be flexible to meet the needs of each individual dispute. A core concept in dispute resolution is the requirement that dispute systems designers "fit the forum to the fuss" by providing resolution processes appropriate to the need of each dispute and disputant. This is simple functional analysis. Indeed, it reckons back to Justice Holmes's discussion of attorneys as problem-solvers. Considering context is simply smart, and it almost always promotes efficacy and efficiency.

Flexibility is especially important for ODR because of ODR's special ability to adapt to a wide variety of resolution processes. Online processes can be customized for a nearly infinite variety of dispute types. Effective and ethical ODR processes must not lock disputants into a one-size-fits-all process that may steer disputants in the wrong direction. The ODR process must be sufficiently flexible and responsive to disputants' needs to change course if need be. Things happen along the way in a resolution process, and ODR must adapt accordingly to ensure party control and comfort.

Takeways

How can we ensure that these ethical guidelines are being followed by programmers and ODR systems designers? It's not as simple as looking at case outcomes. Data transparency is helpful, but sometimes it is very difficult to see what is going on in individual cases by looking at aggregate statistics.

Code audits are one possibility. In the voting technology space, random audits by independent technology consultants are often employed to ensure that there are not systemic biases and fraudulent mechanisms built into voting machines. Similar approaches could work in the ODR context to ensure that ODR software systems are living up to the ethical obligations we set for them.

There is a real risk of private providers of ODR systems creating ODR platforms that have systemic biases. Even if providers first create systems that initially create level playing fields among the parties, their software code may be revised with new biases. This may happen in response to monetary incentives provided by the parties participating in the systems. Continuous monitoring must identify and act when these types of compromises emerge.

External audits are very important for ODR processes. It is imperative to have uninvolved third parties examine the detailed operations of an ODR system and then vouch for the fairness of that system. It is even better if there are multiple auditors, each of whom may represent a different stakeholder constituency within the users of the system. Some of these auditors may be public bodies, whereas other auditors may be private. However, for our ODR systems to retain trust, systematic monitoring from outside auditors to ensure continued adherence to the ethical guidelines described above will be essential.

Of course, such monitoring is not free. Funding will be necessary and thus creative policymakers must craft means for this monitoring to occur in an efficient manner. Nonetheless, ethical standards must be established for design of a global ODR process for consumers. Perhaps a membership organization or professional association for ODR providers could emerge that plays this oversight role, and accepts complaints from users who suspect that these standards are being violated. It will be far more efficient and fair to instill these standards at the outset than to do "clean-up" when things go awry. There will be challenges of course, and no system is perfect. However, keeping these values front and center will be essential if the *New Handshake* is to live up to its promise and potential.

PART

3

Designing the New Handshake

CHAPTER

7

Envisioning a Global Redress System

We have now examined what buyers want, the lessons learned at eBay, the needs of merchants, the obligations of consumer advocates, and the ethical considerations for systems designers. It may seem like a challenge to synthesize all of these elements, or that this is a "pie-in-the-sky" endeavor. However, there are more commonalities than contradictions. In this chapter, we distill these inputs into a set of design criteria that will undergird an effective global ODR system.

It is tempting to slip into cynicism about the fate of consumers on the Internet. Just ask a group of aspiring lawyers to design a consumer protection system and you will hear the negativity: "It is no use," "Consumers always get screwed," "That's just how it is," and "Businesses will always have the power"—as if bad consumer experiences are inevitable and there is no point in trying to fight them. Consumer educators can also fall into an abyss of negativity after years of seeking fairness in the consumer marketplace.

That perspective is wrong. The Internet undoubtedly generates vulnerabilities for consumers, but it also creates enormous opportunities for consumer empowerment. The time is right to take advantage of those opportunities. Merchants, payments providers, consumer groups, regulators, and other policymakers must join forces in addressing this challenge by opening avenues to fast and fair resolutions to online consumers around the world. The world is ready and eager for a global consumer redress system.

There are many considerations to take into account in designing such a system. At first blush, it can seem like the interests of all the players are contradictory and presumably irreconcilable. However, by analyzing the observations, lessons learned, and takeaways from the prior chapters, we can begin to craft a blueprint for a single system that will simultaneously empower consumers with easy access to resolutions, empower merchants with case management tools and improved profitability, and empower consumer protection organizations to be more informed and more effective.

Combatting Asymmetries

One of the factors that leads to pessimism about the potential for buyer protection is the assumption that redress systems will always favor the more powerful player. The dispute resolution field has spent many decades devising techniques that compensate for power asymmetries between parties. Any systems design that will be effective in the consumer context must leverage these techniques in order to create a more level playing field.

As we have discussed previously, consumers buying online suffer today from a variety of asymmetries with merchants that tilt the playing field in favor of merchants. In order to compensate for these asymmetries in our systems design, we must spell out each one and then compensate for it in our blueprint.

First is the volume asymmetry. Most consumers only experience one or two problems with transactions a year. At eBay, 95 percent of disputes filed are from buyers who only report one transaction problem a year, and most buyers report no problems per year. Even if a consumer experiences multiple problems in a single year, most likely they are for purchases on a variety of transaction platforms (e.g., one purchase on Amazon, one purchase on eBay, one purchase on Etsy). In contrast, sellers experience problems on approximately 1 to 3 percent of their overall sales volume. If a seller sells 100 items a month, that means 12 to 36 disputes a year. If he sells 1,000 items a month, that's 120 to 360 disputes a year. If he sells 100,000 items a month—well, you get the idea. This volume asymmetry gives the seller a significant advantage. Sellers are the proverbial "repeat player." This has been a continual complaint with consumer arbitration. A global redress system must combat this by making the process extremely easy to utilize for the consumer. Online consumer redress processes must be very simple and straightforward for the consumer so that consumers are not disadvantaged by their lack of prior experience.

This leads to the second asymmetry: information asymmetry. The seller (or the customer service employees working for the seller) quickly develops a lot of expertise about how the resolution process works. Sellers know what policies govern the outcomes rendered by the process, and they know what evidence will likely sway a decision maker. The consumer likely enters the process with no awareness of how it works, while the merchant enters the process with a long track record of lessons learned. That also means that the consumer must learn the rules as she navigates the process, while the seller already knows how everything is going to proceed. Effective redress must combat this asymmetry by helping consumers leverage information drawn from the experiences of thousands of other buyers. This data must govern not only merchant performance but also prior resolution outcomes.

The third asymmetry is the resource asymmetry. Sellers have the resources to support a long and extended resolution process, while consumers do not. Sellers also have the funds, drawn from many sales over time, to retain counsel and hire dedicated employees devoted to issue resolution. Consumers, most likely, are on their own. If a well-designed and fair redress process is offered to the buyer that nonetheless requires capable representation, understanding of policies and precedents, and presentation of evidence, then the consumer will be at a disadvantage. Consumers simply lack a track record of past cases to learn from. This is often a difficulty for redress systems designed by lawyers because they often assume legal representation is a must. However, this resource asymmetry makes human representation for consumers in individual cases very difficult to achieve. A global redress system must combat this asymmetry by making the process free for all consumers, with no filing fees or costs to engage a neutral mediator or evaluator.

Again, these asymmetries converge to create the "repeat player advantage" noted earlier and in the prior discussion of consumer arbitration. This advantage is at the heart of the power differential between consumers and businesses. Although it is true that this advantage is also endemic in face-to-face resolution processes (not only arbitration, but also the courts), that does not mean it is intractable. We can design a resolution process that simultaneously compensates for the repeat player advantage and gives consumers what they need to be in control of their resolution processes.

It is possible to create a level playing field between consumers and businesses, one that compensates for the three types of asymmetry. The solution is to put the consumer in the driver's seat through the resolution process in order to counteract the procedural advantages enjoyed by sellers as repeat players. It is also essential to provide extensive help content and algorithmic support to counteract the information asymmetry that sellers enjoy. Accounting for these asymmetries in systems design ensures that the buyer is never a passive participant in the resolution process because he has the power to determine the path that the resolution will follow. Furthermore, system monitoring and external auditing can be very beneficial in addressing any repeat player problems that arise.

Business-to-Consumer vs. Business-to-Business Disputes

Because this system is designed to compensate for these asymmetries, it is appropriate for consumer cases only. That means business-to-consumer (B2C) or consumer-to-consumer (C2C) cases should be the only cases allowed into the system. A similar case management architecture could certainly be employed to construct a global business-to-business (B2B) ODR system, though because the parties in a B2B dispute do not suffer from the same asymmetries as B2C matters, the design for that system would need to be fundamentally different.

One of the major sticking points in the UNCITRAL negotiations was the definition of consumer cases vs. business cases. It is not a simple matter to determine if, for example, a buyer is a consumer or a business. Some businesses go online to buy large amounts of goods to stock their brick-and-mortar stores. What is the threshold for those purchases to shift from being a consumer transaction to a business transaction? If I am a large merchant but I am only buying one or two items, am I a consumer? Sometimes it is similarly difficult to determine if a seller is a professional or a hobbyist. If I am selling homemade mittens out of my kitchen, am I a professional seller? What if I become very successful and grow to selling 10,000 mittens a month? At what point do I switch from being a consumer-to-consumer merchant to being a business-to-consumer merchant?

These are questions that can be argued in several directions. Instead of getting sucked into an unresolvable debate, the best way to handle the issue is to come up with a precisely defined delineation that removes the ambiguity. The clearest approach is to pick a transaction value and to say transactions below that value are consumer in nature (and are therefore eligible for this process) and transactions above that value are business transactions and must be resolved through some other channel. This value may be different in different geographies. For example, a $100 purchase in the United States may be considered relatively low value, but a $100 purchase in the Horn of Africa may be relatively high value. This amount may change over time as well, as currencies fluctuate. However, instead of getting hung up on the question of how to effectively triage cases into B2C and B2B buckets, which may in fact be impossible, a delineation like this one is a reasonable approximation and will be easy to implement.

Binding vs. Nonbinding

As was previously discussed, the question of whether ODR systems should deliver binding outcomes has complicated many of the discussions around consumer redress. Indeed, dissention remains regarding the legitimacy of any binding ODR for resolution of B2C claims. There are strong arguments for evaluative approaches: Evaluative outcomes can provide 100 percent closure for case volumes, and they can be extremely efficient to deliver at volume. Parties have also made clear that in some cases what they really want is an evaluative determination. Furthermore, parties gain assured access to remedies from final determinations. This gives disputants an incentive to put forth all their evidence, not holding back facts for future litigation, as may occur in nonbinding facilitative processes.

That said, binding arbitration in face-to-face consumer processes has garnered criticism for undermining the enforcement of statutory consumer protections and other public rights. Some legal jurisdictions even forbid the use of binding arbitrations in consumer transactions, reserving evaluative decision making only for public bodies, like Ombuds Offices or Consumer Courts. In these geographies, requiring ODR outcomes to be binding is a non-starter.

There are ways to deliver evaluative outcomes in a manner that abides by due process and fairness standards, such as reporting, external audits, and other transparency measures. For example, evaluative determinations could be published on a central portal after appropriate redaction of private information. This portal could be easily searchable, and allow consumers and consumer advocates to learn about recently resolved cases. Although some companies may be uncomfortable with such transparency, others would welcome opportunities to garner goodwill and competitive differentiation by complying with consumer protections and providing remedies to deserving consumers.

Ultimately, however, consumers should never be forced to give up their access to a public redress process if they are opted into an evaluative process. Therefore, ODR systems should not block access to the courts for consumers. However, if the systems are well designed, they will resolve 99.999 percent of consumer cases, and those cases will never make it to a court. For the 0.001 percent of complainants who do want to pursue their claim in a court, that right should be preserved, but those cases will be the exceptions that prove the rule.

Individual Claims vs. Mass Claims

One of the recurring criticisms of dispute resolution is that it personalizes systemic problems. If every matter is viewed as a single case, the onus is always on the complainant to report the incident in order to get her particular situation addressed. Complainants often do not have the full picture, as they only know their particular experience, so it is very difficult to connect the dots to identify more systemic problems.

Advocates for mass claim processes (e.g., class actions) argue that resolution processes that require each aggrieved consumer to file an individual case will inevitably underreport problems because some percentage of consumers will not bother to report their issue, meaning the full extent of the situation will not be remedied. Only in a mass claims process, they argue, can the full scope of the problem be resolved.

These criticisms have merit, but they can be remedied through effective systems design. One potential approach can be drawn from Consumer Ombuds offices in the European Union. European countries do not have class actions like we do in the United States, but they are committed to providing strong consumer protection. As was discussed in Chapter 5, one way to achieve this is through a tripwire-like mechanism. The tripwire is triggered when a certain number of cases are filed that fit the same fact pattern.

This mechanism is being used in the United States by the Consumer Financial Protection Bureau (CFPB). As consumers report issues into the CFPB, the CFPB looks for patterns in the reports. If enough similar reports are filed, the tripwire is activated, and the CFPB will notify the business and require them to do an investigation to see how many consumers might have been similarly affected.

Any system design put in place to provide redress for consumers must not work exclusively on a case-by-case basis if it is to be truly effective. Resolutions should always start at the individual case level, but effective data collection can enable pattern detection algorithms that make it easier to detect more systemic issues. Next-generation consumer redress systems must provide resolutions that scale from single issues to mass claims within the same platform if they are to be truly effective.

Trustmarks

Many consumer redress systems have been designed to rely heavily on seals or badges to indicate that a merchant is a trustworthy and reliable transaction partner. In many environments, these trustmarks (e.g., the Better Business Bureau [BBB] seal or the TRUSTe logo) are a valuable tool for businesses looking to establish their legitimacy online. When an e-commerce merchant first enters a market or region, the consumers in that region may have no idea whether it is trustworthy. Trustmarks, particularly those issued by a well-respected organization or public agency, can help new customers to feel that merchant is safe and competent.

Trustmarks are often helpful when e-commerce is new and businesses do not have long track records. Over time, however, trustmarks can start to lose value. It can be extremely difficult to the organizations that issue the trustmarks to manually monitor the behavior of all of the organizations who have opted into the trustmark program. In addition, other organizations may create their own competing trustmarks, which may have different (maybe less stringent) requirements, and then consumers are confused as to which trustmark is more trustworthy. Eventually there may be dozens of trustmarks, and because consumers do not have the time or inclination to research all of them to determine which are best administered, the value of all of the trustmarks goes down.

Eventually, what happens in mature markets is that brands take over for trustmarks. At eBay, for example, there was a proliferation of trust seals from a variety of companies. Some of the trustmarks were well administered, others less so. Some marks promised buyer protection payments should something go wrong, but then later dithered, and the promised protection failed to materialize. Large merchants also began to create their own personal trustmarks, which had graphic designs that were somewhat similar to broader industry-wide trustmarks. Eventually, consumers were so confused that eBay had to ban all trustmarks on eBay listings. Instead of the trustmarks, eBay created its own Trusted Seller program, with a seal that was not inserted into the listing by the seller, but which was controlled by eBay. eBay then used its credibility to back high-performing sellers, which reduced the bad behavior of the trustmark abusers and restored the clarity of the credential. Now, the top trustmarks are actually corporate brands such as Amazon and Zappos. If you want to be sure you will be able to resolve any problems that come up, you shop on trusted sites.

Some trustmarks are bestowed by online review sites like Yelp and TripAdvisor. The argument is that because these sites aggregate information from thousands of users, the four- or five-star rating of a merchant can be trusted as a good indicator of their reliability. The problem is that these sites also have lost meaning due to "flogging" and fake reviews posted by merchants to tout their own businesses. Often, the reviews are not monitored and their veracity is suspect at best. Allowing these unmoderated review sites to serve as a stand-in for more thorough external performance auditing may unintentionally make consumers even more subject to misleading information and bad experiences.

There are ways to do trustmarks well. Private entities must work in collaboration with government regulators and other external auditors to ensure that trustmark systems are ethically administered. However, systems that rely exclusively on trustmarks without ensuring their continuing quality and accuracy may end up generating more consumer confusion over time than they are able to remedy.

Synthesizing Design Criteria

The challenge now is to take all of the conclusions and observations shared so far and to distill them into a plan of action. We have consolidated the conclusions from Part 1 and Part 2 of this book into eight main points that should guide our design efforts:

- Consumers want fast and easy resolutions. They do not want to have to pick up the phone, and they do not want to negotiate for a fair solution. It must be very easy to file a claim. The process needs to be simple to access, free to consumers, and easy to understand.
- The system has to be highly automated. It is the only way to deliver resolutions at scale.
- Consumers want to be treated fairly. They do not need more value than what they are entitled to. They want to be treated like adults and to have their privacy respected.
- Yes, there are bad guys, and the system has to identify the bad guys quickly. However, most problems are not the result of fraud—they are misunderstandings or mistakes.
- The system must be designed to compensate for merchant advantages. It must combat gaming, both from buyers and sellers.
- Merchants must have a clear benefit from participating in the system. They must have a signaling benefit that will create trust with buyers, either through trustmarks or referrals.
- Enforceability is key. Resolutions without consistent enforcement are worthless to buyers.
- The system must be continuously learning. It has to evolve with the times and get smarter the more cases that are run through it.

We will now walk through each of these points and explain how they can best be integrated into an effective ODR systems design.

Consumers Want Fast and Easy Resolutions.

The top observation, heard loud and clear from both consumers and merchants, is that the process must be optimized around ease of use. It must be simple to understand, easy to access, and free for both consumers and merchants. The initiation for the process should reside in exactly the same location where the transaction originally took place: on the merchant's website. The consumer should be easily able to report an issue and get a solution as quickly as possible—instant determination being best, but failing that, a resolution in hours or days instead of weeks or months.

Online guides and wizards should be available to enable consumers to easily educate themselves about their rights, evidentiary obligations, procedural steps, and likely outcomes. Consumers must know exactly what they are getting into when they initiate the process, and they must never feel surprised or misled by a procedural development that they did not know about prior to filing the case.

Furthermore, consumers using the system should not be forced into a negotiation over their rights. Consumers will not be exposed to liability for filing a case in the system, and the system will only receive consumer filings against merchants. In other words, this system is proposed to cover only consumer filings to seek redress, and not merchant filings against consumers.

The consumers who use this process already feel that they have been treated unfairly once, and that is the reason they decided to initiate this process. We must do everything in our power to ensure that they do not feel doubly mistreated by this redress design, and that it is as easy and straightforward as it can be, in order to ensure the consumer feels the process was fast and fair.

The System Has to Be Highly Automated.

The incredible volume of disputes being generated by e-commerce (projected to be more than 1 billion disputes per year in 2017 and beyond) simply cannot be resolved through human-powered resolution procedures. Algorithms are enabling this massive growth in e-commerce transaction volumes, and algorithms are the only way that the disputes arising from these volumes can be adequately managed. These algorithms must be carefully constructed and closely monitored to ensure they are performing appropriately.

It is true that not every case can be effectively resolved by algorithm. The ODR system must work like a filter, where algorithmic resolutions handle the easily resolvable cases, leaving a much smaller volume that requires human attention. Algorithms will handle the triage of cases between automated and manual outcomes.

This approach is the only way to make the system sustainable. The average value of a cross-border consumer purchase is somewhere around $75. It is very hard to imagine a human-powered resolution process that will be able to handle cases at that price point on a cost-effective basis. Even the most junior mediator or arbitrator will expect to be paid $10 to $20 per hour for their services. In a short period of time, the cost of the resolution will exceed the value of the dispute, which makes no sense.

Consumers Want to Be Treated Fairly.

Many merchants feel that consumers have unreasonable expectations and that they are always looking to get more value out of their transactions. It is true that consumers will not say no to an incredibly generous offer from their sellers, but they do not expect such generosity and it will not buy their loyalty. What consumers want is exactly what they were told they were going to get when they agreed to the transaction in the first place.

Consumers do not like to be talked down to or patronized. It is true, as we explained earlier regarding asymmetries, that merchants have more knowledge about e-commerce policies and procedures than buyers, largely as a result of volume. However, that does not mean that consumers are stupid or gullible. The heart of the *New Handshake* is mutual respect, with no attempt to confuse or mislead the other side.

Part of being treated with respect is a commitment to maintaining consumer privacy. Consumers know that businesses are tracking when they make online purchases, use store loyalty cards, or pay for goods or services using their credit and debit cards. Data brokers track spending habits, how long one lingers on a website, consumers' online searching histories, family information, and even postings on social sites such as Facebook. Consumers may tolerate this data collection if it is used to improve their shopping experience, but they are intolerant of businesses treating their private data like another product to be bought and sold.

The System Has to Identify the Bad Guys Quickly.

Systems built under the presumption that all reported issues are fraud will generate frustration and churn. The data shows that problems are inevitable, and the majority are resolvable through direct communication. Consumers and merchants want to have successful transactions, and they can be trusted to do the right thing 99 percent of the time.

Language matters. The tone set in a resolution process is highly correlated to the mindset of the disputants within that process. If the language used within a redress flow presumes ill intent (e.g., filing a "fraud alert" instead of "reporting a problem") then the users within that system will similarly assume that the other side is a bad actor who needs to be punished, as opposed to a transaction partner who is willing to resolve the issue in good faith.

The highest satisfaction and retention numbers are generated in cases where the consumer and merchant can resolve the matter through mutual agreement and direct communication. That is the best outcome for a problem report. If a redress system instead imposes a punitive, victim-offender narrative on problem reports, that will shrink the number of resolutions achieved via mutual agreement and increase the number of cases that are escalated to evaluative outcomes. That will leave at least one party feeling frustrated.

The System Must Be Designed to Compensate for Merchant Advantages.

As soon as a redress system is launched, potential users immediately test it. They may generate a barrage of cases just to try out the different scenarios to see if they can find a seam in the design that can be exploited. It is of utmost importance that the system be designed to combat this type of gaming. When vulnerabilities or perverse incentives are discovered in the flow, they must be addressed quickly.

A redress system may be well designed, easy to use, and impartial at launch, but administrative decisions over time can weaken those characteristics. Every time a policy is reconsidered, redrafted, removed, or strengthened, there is another opportunity for the delicate power balance between participants to be negatively affected. One force that has soured that balance in past processes is the profit motive. Good intentions at launch can come unstuck over the years if the systems administrators pay too much attention to maximizing the revenue stream. This is a challenge for all redress systems, public or private, but private interests may be even more susceptible.

There is no question that private companies should play a part in creating ODR processes, because only they are able to stay abreast of rapidly evolving developments in technology and the global e-commerce marketplace. However, independent evaluators should play a role in ensuring the fairness of these privately created processes.

Tripwires with automatic notification to public regulators and nonprofit oversight organizations can help to provide this outside monitoring function. Once filings cross the specified threshold, regulators may be automatically notified about the nature of the recurring claims, and that may provide possible grounds for an investigation or enforcement action. Also, these tripwires may result in an automatic public notification to inform other consumers of a potential recurring problem. This type of automated action could be especially important where repeated complaints indicate that health or safety issues are at stake.

These automated notification systems could also ease companies' overall dispute resolution costs by making the entire redress process more cost effective and efficient. The trust benefit obtained by participating businesses would provide more than enough economic benefit to justify participation. Furthermore, companies' participation in the ODR process should help them avoid any potential enforcement actions and class claims, and the courts should view participation in externally audited third-party resolution systems as a strong signal that companies are committed to treating their customers fairly.

Merchants Must Have a Clear Benefit from Participating in the System.

One of the big challenges in designing a global ODR system is coming up with branding that will a) communicate to buyers that this system is a safe and effective place for them to resolve purchase problems; b) earn positive notoriety to set it apart from the morass of other redress schemes promoted across the Internet; and c) be cross-culturally valid and appropriate in a wide variety of geographies.

There may be an affiliative halo from participation if respected public and private entities contribute their reputations to the administration and management of the system. Quality merchants will be eager to associate themselves with leading consumer protection and advocacy organizations, even if participation does generate additional responsibilities. But this system cannot turn into an unmoderated and loosely administered trustmark program. The goal is to build a reliable resolution process that consumers will come to understand and utilize, and businesses will realize a trust benefit from their participation. However, the point of the program is not to give out trustmarks; it is to build a new opt-in mechanism to provide buyers a tool that they can utilize should something go wrong.

It is also important for underperforming merchants to be thrown out of the program. The credibility of the system is dependent on strict enforcement of the merchant guidelines. If businesses repeatedly flout the rules and do not resolve buyer complaints yet remain in the system, the trustworthiness of the overall program may be irreparably damaged.

Enforceability Is Key.

Some marketplaces have not done the work required to enable effective enforcement of outcomes. For example, some classified sites do not enable buyers and sellers to hold their transaction partners accountable for performance once the transaction is complete. Users may have no fixed username or account, and once payment is made the consumer may know nothing tangible about the merchant, or may even be unable to contact them with any questions or problems. For example, if an online marketplace provides only a disposable forwarding e-mail address for a transaction partner, and the parties meet in person and make the payment in cash, there is no way to resolve a problem that arises later. Maybe the buyer pays $500 in cash for a laptop, meeting the seller in a parking lot, and then later discovers the laptop is completely nonfunctional. The buyer has no way to contact the seller to ask a question, and there is no way to reverse the payment made in cash. Providing a redress process to the consumer in this context is a waste of time, because even if the outcome is that the consumer deserves a refund, there is no way to enforce the outcome.

Any systems design must build in enforceability if it is to truly meet the needs of consumers. Delivering resolutions that consumers must then find a way to get enforced is not an effective design. Enforcement should be automated, effective, and integrated into the transaction from inception.

The System Must Be Continuously Learning.

Any software designer will tell you that it is almost impossible to get a solution perfect on the first try. No matter how much research, planning, and testing one does in advance of bringing a system live, adjustments are always required. Even if you do happen to get the system exactly right at launch, conditions are always changing, which requires any platform to be able to evolve and adjust if it is to remain effective over the longer term. The value of high-volume caseloads is that those caseloads generate a lot of data, and effective systems designs must be able to learn from that flow of data so that they can continuously evolve and improve over time.

Online dispute resolution systems also have the advantage of being able to engage problems much earlier in the lifecycle of the issue, and early resolutions are the most effective. ODR systems can also offer valuable insights upstream of disputes, so that the transaction environment itself may be able to adjust so as to prevent later misunderstandings which can turn into problems and disputes. This discipline of continuous improvement and learning should be integrated into the systems design from inception to ensure continued relevance and effectiveness.

Takeaways

Building a systems design for a global consumer redress process that can handle such high volumes, cross cultures, and continuously improve is not a simple exercise. There are many considerations that must be factored into the design if it is to be effective over the long term. The lessons we have drawn from the perspectives of consumers, businesses, and consumer advocates have helped us to identify and name each specific consideration we need to keep in mind. We have tested them against the firsthand experience gleaned from the hundreds of millions of cases resolved through eBay's resolution processes, and we have named the ethical criteria that must govern our process. The challenge now is to take these observations and craft a systems design that integrates them all into an implementable blueprint.

CHAPTER 8

The Design: Newhandshake.org

While there is growing consensus that a worldwide redress mechanism is needed to facilitate the growth and expansion of e-commerce, no one has ever crafted an end-to-end systems design for a global, cross-border, high-volume/low-value consumer redress process. In this chapter, we outline our blueprint for a global consumer redress system that is feasible, cost-effective, scalable, and abides by the ethical standards and design constraints we have described.

In this chapter, we introduce our design for a global consumer protection ODR platform that can affordably scale alongside the expansion of global e-commerce. This system is admittedly just an initial proposal for a minimum viable product (MVP), and it will definitely have to evolve and grow over time by adding functionality. However, we believe that this design offers a strong foundation upon which consumer ODR can build over the coming decades.

A Single Platform

The global resolution process must have a single hub that powers the overall system. There will be hundreds of routes into this home base or core platform. These routes in will derive from ODR providers, merchants, and consumer protection authorities around the world. Nonetheless, everything must be centered on a single core architecture. For the purposes of this design, we are going to call that architecture newhandshake.org. This is a fictional website—one that does not currently exist—but we use that domain name in this design to help us get very specific about how the design would work.

Signing Up

Merchants will visit the newhandshake.org site and fill out a form to register in the system. Merchants must specifically agree to the terms and conditions of the program and provide contact information for the individual within their staff who will liaise with any communications from the newhandshake.org administration team.

Once the merchant completes the registration form, they will be provided with a link to their free Resolution Center. This Resolution Center is a cloud-based system through which the merchant can review any problems reported by that merchant's customers through the newhandshake.org system.

The merchant will also be provided with a single line of JavaScript code to place on the home page of their website. This code, when rendered on a web page, generates a small filing button that will look something like this:

THIS MERCHANT IS A MEMBER OF
newhandshake.org
CLICK HERE TO LEARN MORE
OR TO RESOLVE A PROBLEM

This little button looks simple, but it packs a lot of power. It is administered in real time from the newhandshake.org webpage, even though it appears on the merchant's home page. As long as the merchant is in good standing with the newhandshake.org system, the button will appear as it looks above. If the merchant's standing lapses or changes, the button will automatically update on the site. For example, if the merchant is suspended from the program, then the button will be changed to indicate the suspension. If the merchant is upgraded or commended by the program, the button will be upgraded as well to indicate the new status. Every time the merchant's page is refreshed, the new information will appear, and the newhandshake.org server also will note that new view. Real-time statistics quantifying how many times the button is viewed will be shared with the merchants in their Resolution Centers.

The JavaScript behind the button also enables the merchant to share quite a bit of information, at the merchant's discretion, with newhandshake.org once the button is clicked. If the buyer is logged-in when the button is clicked, the merchant will be able to pass along information about the logged-in user to newhandshake.org. If the buyer has an open dispute within the merchant's customer service system or customer relationship management (CRM) system, that information can also be passed along to newhandshake.org. The submission of this information is instantaneous when the button is clicked, and all of it is encrypted to ensure its safety. This is important because it stops third parties from intercepting the data as it is being transmitted to newhandshake.org. To be clear, the submission of this information to newhandshake.org is totally voluntary. Thus, even if the merchant decides not to provide any information through the button, the button will still appear as normal and provide the same functionality to the consumer. Nonetheless, the merchant will be able to access additional features by sharing this information with the newhandshake.org platform.

Note also that the button must be apparent and accessible for consumers on the merchant's website. This means that the button must appear in a prominent location. It will not be adequate to simply bury the button in some fine print, deep in the terms and conditions. The newhandshake.org site will automatically monitor the placement of these initiation buttons and will detect when a button is removed or relocated in an inappropriate way. If the button is moved or removed, the merchant's status in the program will be updated appropriately and possibly deactivated.

This button will work on both mobile devices and full-resolution web browsers. It also can be integrated into mobile apps. This allows it to be fully functional on any wireless device and appear with the correct status even from within third-party code.

Functionality for the Consumer

When clicked, the newhandshake.org button will provide a pop-over window to the existing merchant site. This means that the merchant site is still visible around the outside of the pop-over window. It also allows consumers to close the window at any time and continue at the same place where they were before they clicked the newhandshake.org button. Consumers will be able to submit a complaint at the same place they engaged in the transaction, and then pick right up where they left off after the filing is completed.

When the pop-over window appears, an explanatory message will appear along these lines:

"This merchant, <merchant-name>, is a member in good standing of newhandshake.org, an online problem resolution service. <merchant-name> has committed to quickly and efficiently resolve any problems encountered by their customers. If you would like to learn more about the program, just click here or visit newhandshake.org. If you have a problem to resolve, just click the Report a Problem button below to get started." Below that text will be a button that says, "Report a Problem."

If the buyer decides to visit newhandshake.org or follow the link, he will be directed to the membership page for the merchant in question, which will open in a new browser tab. From there, he can learn more about the newhandshake.org resolution process, learn about the project partners, and review educational materials about his rights and about ways he can avoid encountering problems in his online purchases. This information will be simple, straightforward, and clear, not enshrouded in legalese.

If the buyer clicks the "Report a Problem" button, the text in the type-over window will scroll up and fade out (but not disappear), revealing a question as the new focus for the buyer in the type-over window. Once that question is answered, it will scroll up and fade out slightly, revealing another question. If the buyer so desires, she can move back up to the prior question to review or change her prior responses. In this way, the buyer can explain the nature of her problem through a simple guided filing process.

The questions presented to the buyer will follow this rough structure:

1. What are the details of your transaction (e.g., when was the purchase made, what did you buy)?

2. What kind of problem are you experiencing (e.g., I bought something but didn't get it, I bought something and got it but I'm not happy with it, or I was charged an incorrect amount)?
3. What resolution would you prefer (e.g., I want my money back, I want a partial refund, I want a replacement item)?
4. What e-mail address can we use to contact you about this case?

If the merchant has already provided information about the user logged into his system through the initiation button and his open disputes, the "Report a Problem" process may present that information to the buyers and ask them to confirm it. This would save the buyers from again reporting the details themselves. Convenience is key. The data captured in the intake form will be primarily structured, meaning that the consumer picks information from lists. There will be only one option to submit free-form text to describe the issue in detail. The buyer will also have the ability to upload files or images if, for example, he wants to show how an item was damaged in transit, or why he suspects the item may be inauthentic.

This filing process is designed to take less than five minutes for the buyer to complete. It resides entirely in the type-over window that pops out when the button is clicked. After all the information is submitted, the buyer will see a confirmation message that thanks her for her submission and informs her that she will receive future information via e-mail. Again, when the buyer clicks close, the type-over window disappears and the buyer is right back on the merchant's home page. A confirmation e-mail is immediately sent out to the e-mail address provided by the buyer. From that e-mail, the buyer can indicate if he would also prefer to receive updates sent to his phone via SMS. If so, he can submit the number, receive a text, and enter the code to confirm receipt. The e-mail also includes a case number that the buyer can use to log directly into the newhandshake.org website should he want to take an action outside of the options provided directly to him through e-mail.

The ease of the process is central to empowering consumers. As discussed earlier, consumers lack resources, time, patience, and experience to comfortably assert complaints. They are especially prone to forego complaints regarding small dollar claims because it simply is irrational from a cost/benefit analysis to invest the resources required to assert complaints through traditional face-to-face (F2F) dispute resolution processes. This five-minute process we are proposing makes it feasible to assert these small claims. Moreover, the guided inquiries help consumers from every walk of life and education level comfortably assert their complaints and obtain the remedies they deserve.

Functionality for the Merchant

Once a case is filed by a consumer, the merchant is immediately notified. The liaison specified in the merchant's signup process receives an e-mail notifying the merchant of the new case and asking him or her to log into the Resolution Center for more details.

When merchants log into their Resolution Center, they see a master list of all the cases filed by their consumers. This list is organized by which case most acutely requires the merchant's attention (i.e., a response is due or past due). However, the merchant can sort the list as the merchant prefers or can export the list into his or her own computer or system for further integration and functionality (depending on what additional services the merchant purchases).

The merchant will easily identify the new case in question and click on that row in the list, bringing up a detailed case view of just that single case. All of the information provided by the consumer will appear in that case view. The case view may also include whatever information the merchant decided to include in the JavaScript initiation button the consumer used to report the matter. The merchant can also review any files the buyer uploaded as part of the filing process.

The merchant can then take one of several actions. First, the merchant can enter a response to the buyer's filing, explaining the matter from the merchant's perspective. Second, the merchant can indicate that he will provide the buyer a full refund to address the concern. Third, the merchant can indicate that she has already resolved the matter directly with the buyer, the buyer is now satisfied, and the case should be closed.

All of this functionality is included in the free Resolution Center that the merchant receives just for signing up to be part of newhandshake.org. This alone is an important value-add for the merchant: It saves the costs of establishing another mechanism for resolving a large volume of small-dollar claims. It also helps gain consumer goodwill, by ensuring means for obtaining remedies.

At the same time, merchants who sign up for the base process will have the opportunity to purchase additional functionalities. Some of these functionalities include the following:

- Robust reporting and business intelligence tools to provide real-time data visibility into all incoming problem reports
- API integration so that all filed cases are automatically inserted into the merchant's other customer service platforms (e.g., Zendesk, Desk.com, Salesforce, etc.)
- Policy-based automated resolution tools that can resolve filed cases instantly based on rules entered and managed by the merchant
- Buttons that can be integrated directly into the core of the merchant's platform, on each buyer's My Account page, to capture more specific per-item information
- Integration of other dispute volumes, such as marketplace (eBay, Amazon) disputes and payment (chargeback) filings into the same centralized Resolution Center

The base Resolution Center is free. For many smaller merchants, the free platform will be adequate to deal with the modest amount of cases filed through the program. For larger merchants who require more advanced functionality, these additional features will make the system much more manageable. This is how the ongoing maintenance and operation of the worldwide software system will be funded: through the subscription to these additional value-added services.

Consumer Updates

What separates this proposed process from many generic complaint filing processes is the follow-up. Often, complaint processes cause consumers to feel as though their issues just sank down a black hole, never to be seen again. The newhandshake.org process does not simply end with the case submission. Instead, 24 to 48 hours after the initial filing from the buyer, the newhandshake.org system will send the buyer an e-mail asking if the case is now resolved and how the buyer feels about the transaction. In the interest of saving the buyer time, the notification e-mail will contain several emoji faces that the buyer can click on to indicate his or her current attitude: a happy face, saying everything is fine; a neutral face, indicating neither happiness nor frustration; or a frowny face, indicating dissatisfaction. The buyer will also be asked if he or she wants to close the matter and end communication.

If the buyer selects the happy face and indicates that he wants to end communication, then he will receive a short message congratulating him for getting the issue resolved. The merchant will then receive a message indicating that the case is now closed, and the case in her Resolution Center will be marked with a check mark, indicating a successful resolution.

If the buyer selects a neutral face or a frowny face and indicates that he wishes to end communication, he will be given the opportunity to give the merchant a "strike." This strike, the e-mail will explain, will be a demerit on the seller's account that will be monitored by newhandshake.org. If the seller receives too many strikes in too short a period of time, she will be suspended from the newhandshake.org program. If the buyer decides to proceed with the strike, then the seller will be notified and the strike will be added to her internal records within newhandshake.org.

Notably, the buyers also will have an opportunity to indicate if they feel the seller behaved fraudulently. They also will be able to post a message back to the merchant from the e-mail or SMS they received. As soon as the message is posted, the merchant will be notified and the communication will be visible within the merchant's Resolution Center. This could potentially inspire the merchant to address the complaint or at least consider ways the merchant could improve its products and practices.

Nonresponse

In some cases, a buyer will initiate a case against a seller and the seller will respond to the case, but the buyer will not follow up. Multiple e-mails will be sent to the buyer asking him for his feedback on the case. After three attempted contacts, the buyer will receive a final message saying that his case is about to be closed due to nonresponse, and that as a result no action will be taken against the seller. After a stated time (six or seven days), the case will automatically close and be marked in the merchant's Resolution Center as "timed out." These timed-out cases will not count against the merchant's internal rating in either a positive or negative way.

On the other hand, there may be cases in which a merchant does not respond to a buyer's response. The merchant will be given a timeline for responding (likely two or three days) from when the problem was initially reported. If the merchant continues to provide no response, he or she will be notified that the case will close with an automatic strike against that merchant. Once the timeline elapses, the case will be marked as an automatic strike due to nonresponse and the buyer will be notified. Again, this will be noted in the newhandshake.org system and may potentially lead to merchant deactivation.

Merchant Suspension or Removal

These strikes matter. As noted, merchants who receive a large volume of strikes per transaction will be suspended or removed from the program. The precise numbers are to be determined based on statistical analysis after the system launch. Nonetheless, this threat of suspension should inspire merchants to reply appropriately to consumer complaints. The threat of nonperformance strikes will prompt merchants to take responsibility to their customers, while reassuring consumers that their concerns are being taken seriously.

Such threat of suspension has powerful signaling power. Suspension due to strikes will never be a surprise to a merchant. Merchants will have real-time information regarding their performance on newhandshake.org. They will be well aware of the number and frequency of strikes against them, and they will receive constant notices from the newhandshake.org system about their position. Newhandshake.org will provide merchants with clear guidelines that outline the practices required of newhandshake.org participants, along with graphs in their Resolution Center reporting tabs showing their performance versus aggregated newhandshake.org merchant baselines.

This is not an all-or-nothing system. Instead, there may be cases in which merchants will be placed on restricted status prior to being removed from the system. This will be at the discretion of the newhandshake.org administration team. This restricted status may require several additional obligations from the merchant in order to regain full status. For example, the merchant may be required to provide faster response times to reported problems, additional burdens of proof for marking cases closed, or even the deposit of a reserve payment which can be used to auto-refund consumers for a short period of time. If the merchant is able to manage the complaint and strike rate back down into the acceptable range, these restrictions may be removed. However, if the merchant continues to generate complaints and strikes, the administrators may remove the merchant from the program and revoke her button.

Fees

As was previously explained, newhandshake.org is provided free of cost to all merchants and consumers. The basic technology requires no payment, nor must a merchant put down a credit card number to join the platform. However, if merchant case filing volume exceeds a certain level, then the merchant will be required to pay a periodic fee to continue to participate in the newhandshake.org process. These thresholds will be determined by the Consortium members. Nonetheless, as a rough guideline, merchants who have between 10 and 50 disputes a month will pay $9 per month, merchants who have between 50 and 100 disputes a month will pay $19 a month, merchants who have between 100 and 500 disputes a month will pay $49 per month, and merchants who have 500 and 1,000 disputes a month will pay $99 per month. These fees are modest for most merchants, but they provide appropriate incentives.

The intent is that the vast majority of participating merchants will not have to pay a fee to participate in newhandshake.org. The vast majority of smaller merchants will not have 10 disputes per month; if they do, it should be a relatively simple matter to improve their customer support practices to the point where 10 of their customers do not feel the need to click the "newhandshake.org" button on their home page each month. The newhandshake.org site will provide best practices and advice as to how to reduce filing volumes so that smaller merchants can get below the payment threshold. For larger merchants who will experience higher filing volumes, the benefit of participating in newhandshake.org will more than justify the very modest monthly fees. These low fees will go to support the administrative team, as well as supporting the operation of the consumer advocates who are serving as external auditors.

External Auditor Functionality

Certain external auditors will be provided with their own free Resolution Centers. These external auditors will be selected business associations, regulatory agencies, and consumer protection bodies. These Resolution Centers will not enable the external auditors to communicate with buyers directly. Instead, they will provide real-time dashboards summarizing all of the resolution activity within the newhandshake.org system. For some auditors (e.g., organizations that focus only within a particular geographic region), their Resolution Center will show only the cases within their particular focus area. Other auditors may see only statistics related to a particular purchase type.

Some of these external auditors will come from organizations whose memberships are made up by businesses (e.g., Chambers of Commerce, industry associations). It may be that these organizations eventually require their members to participate in the newhandshake.org system as a condition of their membership. For those organizations, additional tools will be provided to manage the participation of their members and to share information about the performance of the members back to the member management database administered by the governing organization.

Interaction with Legal Remedies

The newhandshake.org system is provided as a purely private redress and resolution system. No outcome delivered by newhandshake.org will prevent a consumer from pursuing other legal action. Consumers remain free to file their claims in court or another legal process. However, merchant participation in the newhandshake.org process should be considered a significant sign of good faith and help ward off unwanted litigation.

Newhandshake.org is a private actor and will not directly engage public legal action. Nonetheless, it will cooperate with any requests from law enforcement regarding an individual case within the resolution system. The intent of this system is to provide timely and effective redress to consumers so that those consumers will not feel the need to pursue their cases in court or even arbitration. And if the consumer does pursue the case in a court, and the merchant has previously met his or her obligation to the consumer through the newhandshake.org process, we anticipate that the judge considering the case will acknowledge the good faith of the merchant's offer for resolution through newhandshake.org (unless it is readily apparent that the merchant was acting improperly). Furthermore, courts will generally give effect to any settlement that the consumers and merchants conclude with respect to a complaint.

Interaction with Credit Card Chargebacks

In some cases, a consumer may file a case through newhandshake.org and indicate that he received a satisfactory resolution, but then later file a chargeback through his credit card issuer requesting a reimbursement for the purchase. The newhandshake.org resolution does not automatically block the consumer's access to his chargeback rights. However, the information gleaned through the newhandshake.org process, including the buyer's indication that he has been fully satisfied, is available to the merchant, and can be submitted as part of a response (or re-presentment) of the charge in the wake of a chargeback filing. This could prevent consumer fraud or "double-dipping."

Over time, as the newhandshake.org system becomes better known, evidence of a successful resolution via the system may gain great force in addressing improper chargeback claims. Nonetheless, consumers who obtain no redress through the newhandshake.org system due to merchants' lack of response or poor response maintain their ability to seek redress to any available chargeback process.

Merchant Appeals

Merchant appeals will be handled by the administration team. Every case that closes with a strike for the merchant is potentially appealable. The merchant will visit the case details page for the closed case and select "appeal outcome" from her actions menu. Once that option is selected, the merchant will be able to fill out a form to explain why she feels the strike was not justified in that particular case. Once the form is submitted, the administration team will review it as queued. The team may then reach out to the consumer in question and ask additional questions of the merchant, who will be able to respond through her Resolution Center. If the administration team agrees that the strike was not deserved, then the strike will be removed and noted as such per administrative review.

Consumers will also have the right to reconsider and remove strikes they have filed against merchants. For instance, a consumer might strike a merchant for item nondelivery, but then the item eventually shows up. If the delay was not the fault of the seller, the consumer will be able to visit the newhandshake.org website to log in with their case identification and fill out a form to request that the strike be removed from the merchant's profile. The system will also ensure that the consumer is not requesting the removal in response to threats or intimidation from the merchant. Once the form is submitted, the administrative team will review the request and carry out the de-scoring if appropriate.

Multilingual Capabilities

The newhandshake.org system will be available initially in English, but it will expand out to other languages over time. The system will not provide machine-translation, but such machine-translation will not be necessary due to the structured nature of the platform. The initiation button will have a setting where the merchant can select the appropriate language for the button, and the button displayed will reflect the merchant's choice. When a consumer clicks the button, the text in the type-over window that appears will reflect the merchant's default language. However, the consumer will have the ability to select a different language for the filing process if he so desires. Because the intake process is structured into a series of questions that the buyer selects from, the information gathered from the buyer can easily be translated from one language to another as needed. The open text information collected from the consumer will not be translated by the newhandshake.org system, but merchants can easily get a rough translation through third-party online translation tools such as Google Translate.

The newhandshake.org Website

The newhandshake.org website will provide a searchable directory of participating merchants. This directory will be searchable by geography, merchant type, and program standing. Each individual merchant will have her own page detailing the information provided during the merchant signup process and the current status of the merchant in the program.

Merchants will achieve different rating levels based on their performance in the program over time. For instance, new merchants may achieve a blue star when they resolve their 50th problem, and more experienced merchants may achieve a platinum star when they resolve their 10,000th problem. The system will not enable public ratings of merchants by consumers, but it will show the current status of the merchant as calculated by the newhandshake.org algorithms and policies.

Consumers will also be able to review help content and utilize diagnosis wizards on the newhandshake.org website. There will be a comprehensive set of resources made available to consumers, governing many areas of online safety and consumer protection. Consumers will also be able to create a login at the newhandshake.org website, using the case number shared with them in the confirmation e-mail received with the initial filing. This will allow consumers to take further actions on their case and post messages. Nonetheless, such login will not be required for every action. Instead, the login will simply be available if a consumer does want to interact directly in the newhandshake.org system.

The Consortium

The newhandshake.org program will be governed by a group of organizations with credibility in consumer protection, merchant quality standards, dispute resolution, and software design. This Consortium may include government regulators, industry associations, and nongovernmental consumer advocates. This Consortium will meet periodically either face-to-face or online to evaluate the continued success of the program and revise its governing principles when appropriate. Each of the Consortium members will serve as External Auditors and will devote some staff time to the monitoring of the overall system. However, the burdens of program administration will not be borne equally among the Consortium members. The technical team will retain the technological responsibility for the operations of the global system, ensuring that it meets all agreed upon service levels, and the administrative team will handle all day-to-day operational responsibilities. The Consortium may also accept new members on a periodic basis, with particular attention being paid to international representation and effective monitoring of merchant performance. The Consortium may also discuss appropriate branding and advertising for the newhandshake.org system, including appropriate partnerships with private and public entities.

The newhandshake.org program will be administered globally by a small team chosen by the Consortium members. The responsibility of this team will be to ensure the continued operation of the newhandshake.org website and to coordinate communication between participating merchants and Consortium members. This team will also supervise the appeals process for merchants.

Mass Claims

By design, each case filed in the newhandshake.org system will be filed one at a time, by an individual consumer regarding a single transaction. However, if there are a sufficient number of claims involving a particular merchant or product, an automatic trigger will alert external auditors. The external auditors may then initiate an investigation of the matter to determine if there is a broader set of consumers who have suffered from the same issue. The external auditor may make this request from within a particular case or set of cases in his or her Resolution Center. The auditor will notify the merchant of the request and provide a certain number of days to respond. The merchant and the auditor can then discuss the matter and agree upon a certain corrective course of action. This may involve the merchant proactively reaching out to all the affected consumers, explaining the situation, and offering an appropriate resolution.

Cooperation with External Systems

The newhandshake.org website will be built on an open architecture that can connect to any external case management system. For instance, the European Union is now launching its own ODR process to handle cross-border consumer complaints within EU member states. However, some of those cases will be filed by EU citizens against merchants outside of the European Union. The newhandshake.org system will provide standard-compliant data exchange interfaces to share information about cases in real time with these other systems. New case filings will come in from consumers reporting issues through the buttons on merchant websites. Nonetheless, other cases may come in via these API connections to external ODR systems such as the EU framework. Merchants will be notified about these cases in the same way they are notified about cases filed directly from the buttons on their websites.

CHAPTER 9

How It Could Succeed and How It Could Fail

We have set forth a design for a global consumer redress process that could work, but at this point the design is only a concept. Many internal and external factors will determine whether this concept will succeed or fail. In this chapter, we call out what steps will be required to make this deliver on its promise, as well as some of the challenges that could doom it to failure.

The *New Handshake* is an ambitious global design for consumer redress. However, it will not be the first time such a system has been attempted. Consider the sophisticated governance systems that undergird the Internet Corporation for Assigned Names and Numbers (ICANN) domain name system or the global Anti-Malware Testing Standards Organization. These organizations also began as ambitious designs, but they were made real by the work of diverse groups of constituents working in common purpose. Both have since enjoyed considerable success and made the Internet safer and more stable. The *New Handshake* could be the next example of this kind of global, multistakeholder, collaborative system.

The success of this effort is not preordained, however. Difficult challenges remain around launching and managing the system; getting the software programmed, debugged, and scaled; spreading awareness among consumers and businesses; refining and improving the platform over time; and ensuring the system lives up to its ethical and trust-building obligations.

In this chapter, we discuss the next steps required to make the *New Handshake* succeed, while at the same time identifying potential risks that could cause it to fail.

Execution

The first step will be creating and testing the software platform that will power the design. Building a system this complex is no simple task. Small missteps at the outset can generate large headaches (and major expense) later on. First and foremost, developers must plan and execute the design in order to turn it into a reliable, working platform. Coders with prior expertise in building platforms like this are essential. They must also work in collaboration with user experience designers to carefully plan the user interaction and visual design, in order to develop a front end of the platform that is responsive, intuitive, and multilingual. DevOps architects must also create servers with flexibility and scalability that will enable the system to grow seamlessly as caseloads increase. The challenges in this phase of the project should not be treated lightly.

At the same time, information security experts must harden the system to ensure it is impervious to infiltration by outsiders. Data security is vital. A large-scale data breach in the platform could be a fatal blow from which the system would not recover. The design is such that the amount of personally identifiable information collected is extremely limited. However, if hackers were able to compromise the system and extract confidential information, that could quickly spell the end of the project. A platform built with an explicit focus on consumer protection is going to be cooked if it cannot protect the information of the users within it. This is not a simple task because new security vulnerabilities are being discovered all the time, so this effort must be focused and ongoing. The price of true information security is eternal vigilance, and it is a price this system will have to pay.

A global, scalable system like the one we have designed will need to interoperate with different platforms, and other ODR providers and dispute resolution organizations will need to be able to connect their systems to this system quickly and easily. This is not an insular redress system; it is designed as an open platform that can coordinate many different end points. Thus, it will be important to have fully documented data exchange interfaces and publicly available data structures, along with standards to enable other platforms to connect in without having to spend too many of their precious development resources. Open architecture and extensibility will be crucial to the success of the effort.

There is enormous risk in a software development project of this magnitude. If the wrong choices are made at the inception of the project (primarily in areas like hosting environments, development languages, open source tools, and the like), it can create long delays, cost overruns, or even risk total failure. That is why it is important to involve experienced technology professionals who can apply their hard won wisdom to these important early architectural choices, so as to minimize risks as the system scales up.

Governance

As more people learn about the system and decide that they want to help, a coalition will need to develop to make the system a reality. It will be important for this group of sponsors and participants to ensure the system is not compromised by narrow, parochial agendas over time, as well as to ensure it remains true to its focus on consumer empowerment and fast and fair resolutions. This group will need to include leading consumer advocacy organizations along with business advocacy groups, trade associations, global e-commerce marketplaces, and public regulators. Participants will need to represent the industry, government, and nonprofit sectors. Some organizations may want to participate only as supporters or simply to stay informed about the challenges encountered. Others may choose to take on more responsibility by assuming technical or administrative roles. Regular meetings will be required to enable the representatives of these various groups to share their perspectives about how the system is operating and to suggest refinements. There will also need to be a system for integrating new members, perhaps allowing at-large participation from individuals unaffiliated with the permanent stakeholder organizations.

The members of this group will serve as the initial ambassadors for the overall effort. It is thus essential that they represent the diverse interests of the full range of participants and stakeholders. Although it is important to keep this group manageable and nimble, the importance of comprehensive representation to effective governance over the long term should not be underestimated.

Some international organizations, like ICANN, have struggled mightily in the area of governance. Turf wars have erupted between for-profit and nonprofit consortium members, and those struggles have led to ill will and extremely contentious meetings. If the consortium does not do a good job establishing a common consensus among all members around how this system will work, what its objectives are, and how it can remain truly ethical and impartial, squabbles within the project governance may block progress and weaken the system over time, perhaps sparking competing platforms. If the consortium becomes divided and the governance becomes muddled and complex, then the project could easily get bogged down in those disagreements, making the system too fragmented to innovate over time.

Project Management

The governance consortium will act more as the overseers of the effort. The day-to-day operations will need to be managed by a core team in charge of keeping the system humming along, addressing issues as they arise. Although this system is designed to be largely self-administering, it will not be sufficient to simply turn the key and "let it go" without close supervision. Instead, ongoing administration is imperative to manage overall case volumes, monitor success, combat downtime, provide support to resolve issues that crop up among users, and respond to unforeseen challenges. Even the hardiest plants need pruning and watering. No system, no matter how automated, can foresee every future circumstance. Although the design is intended to put buyers and sellers into the driver's seat in managing cases from filing to resolution, some processes (like nonperformance strike appeals) will explicitly require human management and oversight.

This small administrative team will grow as needed alongside the expansion of the global system. Over time, this team may diversify into different countries, dividing management responsibilities by geography or language. This team may reside within a global nongovernmental organization (NGO) or a public agency, and it will need to reflect the diversity of the range of case volumes processed within the system. If the design works as intended, this team will not be overwhelmed by a large volume of cases. Still, there must be management oversight and a team available to respond to issues as they emerge, in real time.

The key questions that surround this administrative team include the following: Will they have adequate resources to pay for salaries and ongoing costs? Will they be hosted inside another organization or be free standing? How will the team members be selected? What expertise will they require in order to do their job well? Should there be international representation within the team, if this is to be a truly global initiative? If this team is underresourced or inadequately empowered to make decisions, the *New Handshake* platform risks running off the rails, which would undermine its credibility and increase the risk of failure.

These issues also get to the matter of cost. Human-powered resolution systems are notoriously expensive to run. Many consumer protection organizations are also perpetually underfunded, with far more work to do than hands to do it. If for some reason the automated process at the heart of the newhandshake.org platform in fact requires human attention in order to successfully operate, that will scale costs to the point where it may be too unwieldy to continue operating.

Marketing, Branding, and Education

The well-known refrain from the movie *Field of Dreams* is, "If you build it, they will come." Unfortunately, that is not always true, especially on the Internet. Many great ideas have not survived once they were finally launched online. Even the best built platform can perish if it is not capably marketed because no one will know about it. Education, outreach, and effective branding are essential. This is not an easy task, and it demands professionals skilled in the art of product and Internet marketing. As we have discussed, consumers are already suffering from information overload. This sea of information makes it very difficult to "get the word out" about new services.

The majority of websites fail from apathy, not explicit rejection. It is far more likely for websites to die with a whimper instead of a bang. For instance, it may be that one or more of the target users of the newhandshake.org platform simply does not understand the value proposition. Consumer protection authorities may not see the value in ceding their operations to a global platform that they do not control. Merchants may be reluctant to promote their involvement with a resolution system, or be unconvinced of the economic benefit that such participation could bring to their bottom line. Consumers may not understand what newhandshake.org is intended to do, and as a result, they may not file any cases. Ambivalence from any of these groups could mean that this system never finds traction, and it dies from lack of use.

Accordingly, the coalition and administrative team behind newhandshake.org will need to work diligently in acquiring the initial group of early adopters willing to commit to trying out the new system. They will also need to spend time hand-picking these first participants and helping them along the way. The song rings true: "It only takes a spark to get the fires burning." Indeed, these early adopters will be pivotal as ambassadors who can convince future users of the value of the system. The early adopters' testimonials will be key in convincing future users of the benefits of participation.

Branding, or framing the process for potential users, will also be important. This must coincide with the design of the buttons, the media coverage, and the content that explains how the process works. This must be a collaborative and calculated effort with the aim of attracting early users and moving closer to the tipping point of widespread awareness. Stakeholders and key administrative partners can provide much of this framing at inception, but over time it is likely that professional marketing and branding firms will need to be engaged to further hone the messaging and strategy. (For instance, the name newhandshake.org is pretty clunky—that may be the first thing to go once professional marketers get involved.)

At the same time, students in classes involving dispute resolution and consumer law will be important actors in educating others about this new remedy system. Students are already learning about ODR in schools throughout the world. Students are open to new ways of doing things, especially in obtaining remedies on consumer issues (currently fraught with broken systems that have stymied consumer protection). Students also are aware that the legal and dispute resolution markets are changing, and that they will be eager to be a part of a global online redress system for consumer claims. This could also lead to employment and entrepreneurial opportunities. Accordingly, these students may be ambassadors in adopting and refining the system, as well as empowering consumers with well-crafted information about the process.

Trust

Of course, governance, execution, and marketing are all meaningless if newhandshake.org is perceived as a kangaroo court or does not live up to the ethical standards laid out in Chapter 6. If users lose confidence that the system is transparent, independent, impartial, effective, fair, accessible, flexible, and affordable, that will undermine the entire experiment. Word can get out very quickly if the system is ineffective or perceived to be in the back pocket of one side or the other, and all the marketing in the world may not be able to counteract that perception.

If any of the participants believe the system to be slanted in one way or another, it will quickly lose credibility and then case volumes will decline over time. The most obvious risk may be that merchants perceive the system as too focused on the needs of consumers. The involvement of consumer protection authorities in the administration and monitoring of the system may contribute to the perspective that it is set up only to protect consumers and not to protect merchants. That is why it is very important to get prominent business advocates into the governance group from inception, and to be very responsive to the needs and objectives of merchants in the design and administration of the platform.

Other Risks

There are many other potential risks. Maybe a group of participants figure out a way to game the system to advantage themselves, and the gaming is not quickly discovered and addressed. Maybe the process or user experience design is too complex, and consumers find it confusing or bewildering to navigate the process. If users cannot understand what they are supposed to do, or if they get confused about where they are in the process, they may just give up.

There may also be confusion among users about what exactly newhandshake.org is supposed to be. Is it a trustmark? Is it a small claims court? Most users do not know what mediation is (they confuse it with meditation). If it is just seen as a trustmark, that may alienate other trustmark schemes, and consumer advocates may be reluctant to get involved because they will be worried that participation in the system may be interpreted as a tacit approval or endorsement of a particular business or group of businesses.

Also, users may use the platform to generate abusive, unconstructive feedback. If consumers use the platform to threaten and insult merchants, or maybe even try to blackmail them to provide additional value not included in the original purchase, then the intent of the system will be thwarted. We have seen how communication tools like Twitter and Tumblr have drifted toward threats, insults, and harassment over time. There is a risk that an unmoderated system such as the *New Handshake* platform could move in that direction, and that would drive users away from participation.

Fundamentally, the system will only succeed if it effectively addresses the concerns of the users it is targeting. These concerns may change over time, and the platform must evolve appropriately in response. Both consumers and businesses must always feel that the use of the system is in their best interest. Steering a project like this through the potential pitfalls can be difficult, and only a small percentage of new initiatives successfully make the voyage. However, the need this system addresses is not going anywhere, so there is some margin of error to make a few mistakes without dooming the overall enterprise.

CHAPTER

10 Case Studies

The case studies in this chapter are meant to give the reader a better sense of how this design for the New Handshake *would work in practice. Consider how such an ODR system could work for different kinds of consumer and merchant problems. It is imperative to use real-life fact patterns to see how different types of issues would play out from the perspective of all the different users of the platform: consumers, merchants, and administrators. Educators may wish to expand these case studies in guiding students through exploration of dispute resolution in the digital age.*

Case 1: The Missing Dog Toy

Anna visits dogtoys.com to buy a new squeaky duck toy for her Chihuahua, Rafael. She finds the perfect model of toy, a yellow duck wearing sunglasses, just like the toy that Rafael had joyously chewed up and destroyed several months earlier. Anna adds the toy to her shopping cart and hits *Submit.* She immediately gets a confirmation e-mail, so she shuts down her computer to go watch Downton Abbey.

Two weeks later, while she is standing in line at Starbucks waiting for a latte, Anna realizes that the squeaky duck toy has still not arrived. She goes back to her e-mail to find the confirmation message she received when she made the initial purchase. The confirmation does not include any shipping or tracking information, merely an assurance that the item will be shipped as quickly as possible. Anna checks her credit card statement via the online portal and confirms that the payment did go through.

Anna goes to the help section of the dogtoys.com website to look for ways to find the shipping status of her purchase, but after much clicking around, she can find nothing on the website that seems relevant to her situation. There is one e-mail address specified for use by customers who are asking about the availability of a particular item, so Anna sends an e-mail to this e-mail address along with the order number she received after making the purchase. She politely asks when her purchase is likely to arrive.

Three more days pass, still with no response. Anna sends another e-mail, this one a little more aggressive in tone. Still not a peep. Anna combs again through the dogtoys.com help section looking for a phone number or even a street address for the business, all to no avail. A Google search shows that other purchasers have reported problems with their purchases from dogtoys.com, and that some of those other buyers have solved their issues through newhandshake.org. Anna decides to give it a try.

Anna revisits the dogtoys.com home page and sees the button there that indicates dogtoys.com is a participating merchant in newhandshake.org. Anna clicks on the button and is presented with a pop-up window that explains what newhandshake.org is and a short form asking her to provide an e-mail address, the date of her purchase, the order number, and a description of the problem she is experiencing. The form also asks what kind of redress she would prefer in this situation. Anna explains that she still has not received the squeaky duck she purchased and that she would like a confirmation that the item will be delivered soon or a refund.

Mike Green, the owner of dogtoys.com, receives a notification in his e-mail from newhandshake.org telling him that a new issue has been reported via the newhandshake.org button on his home page. Mike clicks the link in the notification e-mail and views the case within his Resolution Center. In the case is the information that Anna submitted about the missing squeaky duck. Mike checks the order number and looks it up within his customer service platform. According to his records, the squeaky duck was sent out three days after the purchase was made. There was a small delay due to a backlog in shipping, but nothing that would explain why the item hadn't arrived after two weeks. Mike's customer service platform also has a tracking number that shows the item was sent out via the U.S. Postal Service (USPS). Mike enters the tracking number on the USPS website and sees it is marked as being in transit, currently located in the post office closest to Anna's house.

Mike then e-mails Anna directly at the e-mail address she provided in her filing form and apologizes for the delay in delivery. He also includes the USPS tracking number in the e-mail. He explains that for some reason the item is still sitting in the post office, and it has not yet been delivered to her house. Mike asks if Anna would be willing to go by the post office to inquire about the item.

The next day, Anna goes to the post office with the tracking number Mike provided. After standing in line for 10 minutes, Anna explains the situation to the counter agent. The agent then pokes around in the back of the post office and discovers Anna's box sitting on a shelf above the sorting area. The agent then brings out the item to Anna and explains that it was likely that the postman attempted delivery while Anna was not home and then brought the item back to the post office, forgetting to attempt redelivery the next day.

Two days later, the newhandshake.org platform e-mails Anna and asks if the issue she reported has been addressed to her satisfaction. The e-mail offers three buttons: a smiley face button, a neutral face button, and a frowny face button. Anna clicks the neutral face button. She then has an opportunity to explain why she was neutral about her transaction on dogtoys.com. Anna explains that the delay in delivery was not the fault of the website, but that she found it very difficult to contact the merchant to get a response. Newhandshake.org then asks Anna if she would like to give dogtoys.com a nonperformance strike for this transaction, and Anna indicates that she does not want to do so.

Mike Green is notified by e-mail that the consumer issue has now been closed in his newhandshake.org Resolution Center. When he logs in to review the closure reason, he sees Anna's comment detailing her frustration in trying to find contact information for someone at dogtoys.com. Mike also sees that Anna rated her transaction with a neutral face but that she decided not to leave a strike. Mike then updates the help system on his website to offer a phone number that will ring to his office should any of his customers encounter a similar problem in the future. Mike also sends Anna an e-mail containing a gift code for $5 off of a future purchase, along with a message apologizing for her frustration and indicating that the phone number has been added to the dogtoys.com help system in response to her feedback.

Analysis

This is an "item-not-received" dispute. Anna paid for the toy, but it did not arrive. Although this problem was fairly simple to resolve (the box was just stuck in the post office), the lack of responsiveness from the seller led to frustration on the part of the buyer. It added to Anna's frustration that she could not figure out how to get her issue addressed after consulting the help content on the dogtoys.com site. Nonetheless, it turned out that the delay was not the fault of the seller in question (Mike). The newhandshake.org button on the home page of Mike's site gave Anna another option to get a response, and that notification raised the issue to a level that hit Mike's radar. The newhandshake.org Resolution Center also made it easy for Mike to quickly diagnose the problem and explain to Anna how to best get it resolved. The frank feedback from Anna also incentivized Mike to rethink the content on his site, which means that future buyers will not experience the same frustration.

Case Study 2: The Bad Hair Day

Grace Stewart was having a "bad hair day." Her hair was flat, lifeless, and would not hold a curl. She looked (and felt) bad about herself with her hair looking so stodgy. Grace had purchased plenty of curling irons at the local beauty and big-box stores, but all the irons she bought did not do the job. Grace therefore searches online for better curling irons and finds a site that looks perfect: CurlyQ.com, which boasts that "their curling irons could bring volume and gorgeous curls to even the flattest hair." The photos on the website are of women (of course, gorgeous models) with great curly hair with amazing volume. Grace thinks, "Well, it's worth a shot."

The CurlyQ website seems legitimate. It has the "https" address that Grace always looks for, so she feels comfortable putting in her credit card number. The site also says that their curling irons come with a "money back guarantee."

Relying on that promise, Grace buys one CurlyQ curling iron for $19.99, plus shipping and handling of $8.99.

Grace receives the curling iron a few days later and eagerly plugs it in to give it a try. Grace is dismayed, however, when it does not heat up. The "on" light comes on weakly, it seems, but even after five minutes the iron is only warm. She plugs it into various outlets around her house and gets the same result. She even tests her outlets with other appliances and confirms that her outlets are working fine. It is clear that the curling iron is the culprit. Worse yet, Grace has a date for that evening and had been hoping to use the curling iron to spruce up her hair for the big night out. Now she is stuck again with lifeless, flat hair. The thought fills her with aggravation.

The next day, Grace goes back to the CurlyQ website and finds a phone number for their customer service team. She dials the toll-free number and is dropped into a phone tree. She presses a few numbers to try to get to the right place, but they put her on hold; after 20 minutes, she hangs up out of exasperation. She then finds an e-mail address to CurlyQ's customer service and sends a strongly worded message demanding her money back. Within a few hours, she receives an automated e-mail from donotreply@curlyq.com stating: "We are sorry, but due to stock limitations, defective item replacements may take up to 4–6 weeks to complete."

At that point, Grace is ready to post negative reviews of CurlyQ on every social media outlet she can get her hands on. That night, she starts badmouthing CurlyQ to her friends over drinks at a local pub. One of her friends asks her if she thought about getting a refund through her credit card company. Grace had heard one can get a "chargeback" from her credit card company, but she is worried about going that route in case it harms her credit rating. She also worries that there could be a dispute about how much she should get back for the faulty item, since the cost of the item ($19.99) was separated out from shipping ($8.99); ultimately, she really wants all of the $28.98 back. Grace even feels entitled to some additional money to account for her annoyance, and she knows the credit card people would never offer her that.

As the friends discuss Grace's dilemma, Grace's friend Ted opens up the CurlyQ site on his phone and sees the newhandshake.org button on the home page. Ted suggests Grace file a case through that button. The next day, Grace goes back to the CurlyQ website and finds the button. She sees that CurlyQ.com is a participating merchant in newhandshake.org, and Grace reads up on how the program works. She then clicks on the button and is presented with a pop-up that explains what newhandshake.org is, and a short form asking her to provide an e-mail address, the date of her purchase, the order number, and a description of the problem she is experiencing. The form also asks what kind of redress she would prefer in her situation. Grace explains that she received the curling iron but it was defective and that it would not get hotter than slightly warm. She also adds that the advertisements promised a "money back guarantee" and that she wants her full $28.98 back. She also mentions that she is considering filing a chargeback through her credit card.

Kristi Dever, the Head of Customer Service at CurlyQ, then receives a notification in her e-mail from newhandshake.org telling her that a new issue has been reported via the newhandshake.org button on the CurlyQ home page. Kristi clicks the link in the notification e-mail and views the case within the Resolution Center. In the case is the information that Grace submitted about the defective curling iron. According to Kristi's records, the curling iron was marked "tested" by her supplier and shipped out as "working condition" (although Kristi is well aware there have been some inconsistencies in the items delivered by their manufacturer as of late). Nonetheless, Kristi e-mails Grace directly at the e-mail address Grace provided in the filing form. Kristi apologizes for the problem but notes that the curling iron was tested to be in working condition before it was shipped. Kristi suggests that Grace should check her electrical outlets to make sure that they are working correctly. Kristi does note, however, that if Grace is still unhappy, CurlyQ will stand behind the money back guarantee and provide a refund of the $19.99 if Grace sends back the curling iron at Grace's cost.

When Grace gets the e-mail, she is livid. She could not believe that Kristi did not immediately refund all of her money, including shipping, or send a new curling iron. Grace thinks to herself, "What about 'the customer is always right'?!?" Moreover, Grace was not about to spend the money to send back the curling iron (especially because she already spent $8.99 for shipping in the first place).

Grace receives an e-mail from newhandshake.org asking how she would like to proceed. Grace immediately clicks the frowny face, indicating that she is unsatisfied with the resolution offered by CurlyQ. She then has an opportunity to explain why she was unhappy about her transaction on CurlyQ.com. Grace notes that CurlyQ did not offer a full refund that included shipping and complains that CurlyQ had the gall to insist that the product was not defective. Grace is also given a chance to upload a video of the curler malfunctioning, which she does with relish, capturing the video on her cell phone. She tapes herself plugging the iron in, it turning on weakly, and then holding the heating element to show how it does not even get warm. Grace even plugs in another device to show that the outlet is not the problem. Once the video is uploaded, newhandshake.org then asks Grace if she would like to give CurlyQ another chance to make it right or simply give CurlyQ.com a nonperformance strike for the transaction. Grace indicates that she would like to continue the discussion.

At that point, newhandshake.org informs Kristi that Grace is not happy with the proposed resolution. The information submitted by Grace is all available in the CurlyQ Resolution Center, including the video. Kristi watches the first two minutes and then skips ahead to see Grace holding the heating element for a full 30 seconds while the unit is on. It is obvious she got a bad unit, so Kristi immediately capitulates.

Kristi sends an e-mail and apologizes to Grace for not believing that the iron was broken. Kristi offers to send Grace the full $28.98 or a new CurlyQ Deluxe curling iron that sells for much more than the standard iron that Grace had originally purchased (and which does not suffer from the same manufacturing issues).

Being online at the time, Grace gets the e-mail immediately and only has to pause for a moment to think about it before deciding to give the new iron a try. Grace had seen the Deluxe advertised but opted for the lower-end $19.99 iron due to her limited budget. She was actually looking forward to trying the new iron and Kristi's apology and willingness to work through the dispute in the online mediation helps to ease her fears that CurlyQ is fraudulent top to bottom.

The Deluxe curling iron arrives a few days later, and Kristi covers the shipping. Grace plugs it in, and it works great. It heats quickly to a perfect temperature, and it provides the exact flip Grace wants in her hair. It also adds unexpected volume and shine. The Deluxe iron has a special coating as well that protects Grace's hair from heat damage. Looking at the results in the mirror, Grace cannot help but crack a smile. She cannot wait for her next date.

Kristi is notified by e-mail that the consumer issue has now been closed in her newhandshake.org Resolution Center. She also sees that Grace has posted satisfaction with the resolution and added a positive review about CurlyQ due to its willingness to find a solution. However, Kristi realizes that CurlyQ has a quality issue with her manufacturer. She sends a strongly worded memo to her product testing department telling them they need to up their game. The individuals who were supposed to test the irons often skipped a few under the assumption that they would all be fine. In other words, the employees had become lazy and their training was lacking. Kristi raises the issue with her boss, sharing Grace's video, which leads to a new training program for the product testing department employees and an incentive system through which employees could earn gift cards to local restaurants for catching defective products before shipment.

Analysis

This is a "defective item" dispute. Grace paid for the curling iron, but it did not work. While the problem seemed clearly the fault of CurlyQ in Grace's eyes, it was not clear to Kristi. How was Kristi to believe that the iron did not work when her testing department let it go out as "working condition"? For all Kristi knew, Grace was lying in order to get back money and keep the iron for free. Kristi also did not fully appreciate how shipping costs make all the difference when asking for a customer to send back a defective item to get a refund. On the other hand, Grace did not understand why it would be difficult not to simply send her the $28.89. Moreover, her anger caused her to stop direct communications after Kristi's initial offer, instead of considering that there are other ways of showing proof of product defect than sending the product back. It took the video to get both of them on the same page.

The result was a win-win. Grace finally found a product to address her bad hair days, and CurlyQ avoided a nonperformance strike and some hits on social media. The frank discussion also incentivized Kristi to rethink the training and incentive programs in the CurlyQ product testing department. Her company would have suffered more complaints if it continued to send out bad products due to poor testing. The new training program should also help stop shipment of curling irons that could be safety hazards.

Case Study 3: All That Shimmers Is Not Gold(fish)

Yuri Rabinovich logs on to freelancehub.com and purchases website building services from a freelance web designer based in the Czech Republic. Yuri is starting a club for goldfish appreciation, and he wants the site to look top notch. The freelancehub.com website asks Yuri to provide a detailed description of the website he is looking to build, down to his preferred color scheme and typeface. Yuri spends more than an hour filling out all of the questions asked by the intake process; at the end, he feels certain that the freelance designer has a good idea of exactly what Yuri is looking for. Yuri pays $500 into the escrow account at freelancehub.com and awaits the first update from the designer.

One week later, the freelance designer e-mails Yuri and says she has the first version of the mockups of Yuri's new website now available. Yuri logs into Skype with great excitement, eager to see what the freelancer has come up with. However, once the website mockups appear on Yuri's screen, he is immediately disappointed. The photos of goldfish have none of the golden shine he was looking for, and the water seems murky and lacks depth of focus. All in all, the website seems amateurish and crudely made, and it does not even use the turquoise color scheme that Yuri had requested when he first filled out the form on freelancehub.com. Yuri communicates his disappointment to the freelancer, and the freelancer reassures him that the next revision will be far more professional. The freelancer also asks Yuri to release the first $250 payment from the escrow account to pay for the work completed to date. Putting his reservations about the work aside, Yuri relies on the freelancer's assurances that the next deliverable will be more professional and releases the first $250 payment.

Two weeks later, the freelancer indicates to Yuri that the website is near completion. Yuri is surprised by this because he was expecting another round of mockups before the design was to be finalized. Yuri logs into Skype and again is frustrated by the amateurish characteristics of the website presented. It appears the freelancer has moved beyond a mockup stage and is very close to launching this design as the final website deliverable. Yuri communicates his frustration again to the freelancer, noting that he did not approve of mockups from the prior call and that he had expected that the freelancer would design a new set of mockups prior to creating the fully realized website. The freelancer indicates that she had a different recollection of their prior conversation and that Yuri had approved the mockups she had initially shared by releasing the $250 payment. This freelancer then indicates to Yuri that she only has one more hour that she can devote to this project and that she does not have the time remaining to change the website design in question. Yuri then indicates that he is not satisfied with the final deliverable and that he will not approve the final $250 payment based on the work completed. The freelancer indicates that she is similarly frustrated and that she will communicate her frustration to the administrators at freelancehub.com.

One week later, Yuri receives an e-mail from the freelancer with a zip file containing all of the files and designs for the new website. Yuri reviews the files and confirms they are the design that he is unwilling to accept. The freelancer then files a request on freelancehub.com to receive the final $250 payment. Yuri takes no action in response to this request. The freelancer then files a complaint with the job management team at freelancehub.com requesting that the final $250 be released from the escrow fund because the freelancer provided all of the agreed-upon deliverables to Yuri for the project.

Yuri then clicks on the newhandshake.org button found in the help center of freelancehub.com. Yuri explains that he was dissatisfied with the work performed by the designer and details the discussions they had around the release of the first escrow payment. Yuri indicates that the reason he did not approve the final payment is because he is dissatisfied with the work and feels it is not of acceptable quality.

An agent working with the job management team at freelancehub.com sees Yuri's report and then convenes an online dispute resolution process between the freelancer and Yuri within the newhandshake.org Resolution Center. All of the details shared at the beginning of the project are included in the online resolution space so that Yuri, the freelancer, and the agent can all review the original agreement. The agent then asks questions of both Yuri and the freelancer to focus on what aspects of the final deliverable Yuri finds unacceptable. Yuri points to the information he had provided in the initial questionnaire around color scheme and typeface and indicates that the final product did not make use of Yuri's criteria. The freelancer initially argues that there was a later agreement not to use these criteria in the final design, but after some conversation, agrees that the final design should be refined to integrate the suggested color scheme and typeface.

The agent then notes that freelancehub.com can provide a new designer to make the requested revisions. Freelancehub.com will cover the cost of this new designer. The agent then asks Yuri if he would release the final payment if this new designer is able to refine the final website to Yuri's satisfaction. After some consideration, Yuri agrees to the arrangement.

One week later, freelancehub.com sends Yuri the revised files that have been refined by the new designer. Yuri finds the design much more professional and in line with his initial expectations as to the quality of the final website. The water is clear and turquoise, and the goldfish pictures really pop. It is like looking into a high-end fish tank in a swanky hotel lobby. Yuri then indicates to the mediator that he is willing to release the final escrow payment, on the condition that he would like to leave a review for the initial freelancer indicating his dissatisfaction with both the process and the work delivered. The agent sends Yuri a form where he can enter this final feedback. Once Yuri has completed the evaluation of the freelancer and confirms his feedback appears on the freelancer's profile page, he releases the final payment from escrow and the case is closed.

Analysis

Service disputes are different from tangible item disputes in several important ways. First of all, a return is not possible in most service disputes. The work done by a freelancer cannot be "returned" like a tangible item. In the case above, once the freelancer had built the website, the hours of labor were expended, and any change would require even more hours of labor. Another challenge is that the quality of the final deliverable in a service transaction may be subject to opinion, making rule-based or policy-based outcomes difficult to implement. Online intermediaries, like freelancehub.com in this example, have a strong incentive to provide fast and fair resolution processes to overcome concerns on the part of customers that it will be difficult to obtain redress if the final deliverables are unsatisfactory. Escrow-based payment systems can address some of this hesitance, because consumers will always have the right to release each payment based on their satisfaction. But negotiating over escrow can be aggravating for consumers, and may discourage them from using the service in the future. By giving the consumer an easy path to redress through the newhandshake.org button, and by stepping up to provide a new freelance designer to ensure the consumer is satisfied, freelancehub.com quickly addresses Yuri's frustration and gets him the outcome he wants, which means he is much more likely to return to purchase more services in the future.

Case Study 4: Prepaid and Pre-Spent

Paul Matheson has a daughter, Patty, who is going off to college out of state. Patty is not very responsible with money, but she has been relentlessly begging Paul to get her a credit card. Paul does not want to get her a regular credit card, however, because he worries that Patty will run up debt and get in over her head. Paul therefore goes online to look for a prepaid card that allows one to load a certain amount onto a card that his daughter can use like a credit card. Such prepaid cards may be beneficial for college students like Patty because they are accepted like a credit card, but they cannot generate any debt. They also may teach kids good budgeting practices because they cannot go over the specified amount.

After some searching, Paul finds a website called PrepaidsRus.com. The website boasts that their cards are "fee free" and "accepted at all stores and online merchant sites that accept Visa cards." Lured by these statements, Paul enters his information and purchases a prepaid card in the amount of $500 for his daughter's use. In the process, he does not see any notices about fees or additional costs above the $500 that he loads onto the prepaid card.

A few days later, Paul gets the prepaid card in the mail. He gives it to Patty before she leaves for college. He explains that she must use it sparingly because it cannot be used for any amount over $500 and must last her through the first two months of school. Patty complains that it will not be enough money, but Paul is adamant that it is all she will get for the two months; if she wants more money, she will have to get a campus job.

Four weeks pass, and Paul gets a call from Patty. She is crying because the card is already out of money, but she swears that she only spent $450. Skeptical, Paul asks for a tally of all she purchased on the card, supported by receipts. This infuriates Patty. How can her Dad not trust her? She yells in a rage, "Go ask the card company if you do not believe me!" She then hangs up and cries.

Paul feels terrible, but he wants to know if she really is telling the truth. So, Paul goes back to PrepaidsRus.com to see how he can get a statement showing what was spent on the card and where that money was spent. Paul finds an account link and signs on to get the statement. He sees that Patty spent a total of $450 in various transactions at the supermarket, restaurants, and Amazon.com. Nonetheless, the card showed no money remaining for use. Patty was not lying! The card was empty although she only spent $450. This was because various fees ate into the card balance. There were maintenance and per-use fees that added up to $50 and emptied the card. Paul calls Patty and apologizes for not believing her. She forgives him but is still hurt over the incident.

Now Paul is angry with PrepaidsRus.com. He goes back to the website and looks for customer service contacts, to no avail. However, he notices the newhandshake.org button in the help center of the website. Paul explains in the intake form that he wants to contest the $50 in fees assessed on the prepaid card he purchased because he was never notified about the fees and relied on the website's statement that the cards were "fee free." Paul emphasizes that he would not have purchased that prepaid card if he knew about the fees. He would have been better off simply giving Patty $500 in cash!

An account representative at PrepaidsRus.com sees Paul's complaint and then invites Paul into a chat process within the PrepaidsRus.com Help Center. The account representative attests that the contract terms provide notice about the fees and attaches the contract terms. Paul contests this because he never saw the information on the website. He also never read the fine print of the terms and conditions agreement and explains to the representative that it would be unfair to hold him to $50 in fees on a $500 card. He also again emphasizes the "fee free" promise on the site. The account representative continues to emphasize the legal agreement, denying any misrepresentation, and ends the chat.

Paul finds the newhandshake.org button on the front page of the PrepaidsRus.com website and reports a problem. There is no follow-up communication from PrepaidsRus.com. Two days later, Paul gets his follow-up e-mail from newhandshake.org and immediately clicks on the frowny face in the newhandshake.org, adding a nonperformance strike against the company. He explains that PrepaidsRus.com charges high fees on its cards despite its website promise of being "fee free."

Meanwhile, many other consumers who have had similar experiences add strikes for PrepaidsRus.com. They report similar stories due to false advertising about their fees. This triggers an investigation by a state consumer protection office. The office sends a notice to PrepaidsRus.com asking for their advertisements and explanation regarding the fees.

This captures the attention of the CEO of United Financial, the parent company of PrepaidsRus.com, who is unaware of the complaints or discrepancy between the contract fees and advertisement on the website. PrepaidsRus.com is actually a very small division of United Financial. It generates fairly healthy profits, but it is a relatively small-volume business. The CEO replies immediately to the notice from the public consumer protection authority and requests a meeting to discuss how the company can rectify the situation without incurring large fines or other penalties. The authority responds and representatives meet with the CEO to find a solution.

The PrepaidsRus.com CEO agrees to pay back all of the fees it collected plus interest to the harmed consumers and places additional money in escrow to be paid out to consumers who had not yet complained but suffered the unadvertised fees. The CEO also revamps the website and deletes any promises about being "fee free." Instead, the site includes a very clear notice of the fees, which are lowered to be within reasonable boundaries as agreed by the public authority. The authority also insists that PrePaidsRus.com hold special training sessions for its account representatives to be sure that they handle these complaints properly and provide notice about fees at the point of sale. The state authority therefore does not assess further penalties or fines.

Paul receives an apology, along with $50 plus interest, from PrepaidsRus.com. He signs the check over to Patty, who is very happy to have the cash.

Analysis

Fee disputes regarding financial products purchased online are tricky. It may seem like an easy dispute to handle through typical chargeback arrangements for credit cards. However, prepaid cards are different and do not come with the same rights. Also, they are often sold online and consumers' only access to the company may be through the website where the consumers purchased the card. Simple customer service links for e-mail or telephone support may seem sufficient, but often such avenues fail. The e-mail reply centers may be staffed by untrained personnel. Also, consumers are often skeptical of products like prepaid cards; therefore, a company's affiliation with newhandshake.org could garner the consumers' trust—and serve as a meaningful competitive differentiator.

Of course, no company wants to be subject to an enforcement action from a government consumer advocacy organization. As the above scenario indicates, company leaders may not even realize that their companies have problems. The CEO of PrepaidsRus.com does not handle the advertisements or realize how his sales team might be luring consumers into believing that the prepaid cards do not involve fees. The CEO in the scenario thought that everyone was aware of the contract terms. He also failed to fully appreciate how repeated transaction fees could eat away the card balance—even on cards for only $500. The notice from newhandshake.org's trigger to the state authorities allowed the CEO to be proactive to find a solution and avoid further penalties. It also allowed the company to develop better business practices that will help regain goodwill that was lost due to the many unhappy customers who complained about the fees.

Case 5: It's in the Bag

Frank Cortes runs an online site called canvasbags.com. Anyone who wants to receive a custom printed canvas bag can visit Frank's home page, upload their design, and get an immediate quote for the number of bags they are looking to buy. Frank has run this business for more than 15 years and prides himself on his five-star customer rating. Most of Frank's purchases come from word-of-mouth referrals from past or current customers to new customers. Frank has had a few unreasonable buyers over the years. However, with clear communication and transparency about how the bag printing process works, Frank has learned how to avoid most of the trouble spots that can crop up in his line of work.

Frank learned about the newhandshake.org process at an industry convention for the Screen Printers Association. Because Frank puts such a high priority on taking care of his customers, he was immediately intrigued. As soon as he returned from the conference, he consulted the brochure that he had picked up and visited the newhandshake.org website, where he signed up for a free account. Frank filled out the intake form to sign up, agreed to the terms and conditions, and provided contact information about himself and his business. Once confirmed, he was given a free Resolution Center (located at canvasbags.newhandshake.org) and a single line of JavaScript code that he could place on his home page to display the newhandshake.org button. It took him about 15 minutes to get it live, and then there it was in the lower left corner of his site, indicating his commitment to take care of his customers.

The next day, Frank noticed a bump in his new buyer visits to canvasbags.com. When he looked at his referral links to his home page in his site metrics, he saw that many users were coming to him from online directories that listed merchants who were participating in newhandshake.org. Frank also got some nice mentions on social media from customers observing that canvasbags.com had opted in to newhandshake.org. Frank felt pride that he was included in a list of worldwide merchants who committed themselves to taking good care of their customers. Even though it was early to tell, he thought it was bringing him new customers.

A year later, Frank was visiting his family in Buenos Aires when he slipped and fell walking down a wet staircase near a waterfall in a national park. After limping back to the tourist bus, his ankle started to swell severely, and he was rushed to the hospital where they confirmed that the ankle was broken. Because the break was severe, it required surgery to insert several screws to help the bone to heal correctly. Frank had to check into a residential hospital down the street from his sister to recuperate. Frank was not concerned about the business because he was confident that his foreman, Charlie, who had worked with Frank for years, would be able to keep up with incoming orders.

After three weeks in Argentina, Frank returned to Tallahassee, still on crutches and wearing a cast. He called the office to check in, but it went to voicemail several times. Frank was not that concerned, but he did think it was strange. The next day, he had his nephew drive him into the office and he was very dismayed with what he found. Everything was a mess. There were half-completed jobs in the screen-printing frames, along with a morass of invoices and work orders scattered around on the tables. Charlie was nowhere to be found. An hour later, Evan (one of the interns) showed up at the front door. Frank quizzed him about the state of the office, but Evan claimed to not know anything. He said that Charlie had been in and out of the office, but that Evan had not seen him for several days.

Frank logged in to the website management system and saw there was a backlog of more than 150 customer inquiries. Many of the messages said that they had completed an order of canvas bags but that they had not showed up at the time and date the website had indicated the job would be completed and delivered. It was clear that the website had continued to take orders while Frank had been in recuperation but that many of the orders had not been completed, and the customers had not been informed of any change in the status of their order. Frank was very upset. The next day when Charlie came into the office, Frank confronted him about the backlog orders. Frank found Charlie's attitude flippant and dismissive. As a result, he fired Charlie on the spot.

Frank immediately got to the task of dealing with the backlogged orders. He e-mailed every customer waiting in the queue to inform them of what had happened. Frank also apologized for the lack of communication. For several of the customers who had been waiting the longest, Frank offered full refunds if the customer wanted to cancel the order or significant discounts if the customer still wanted to proceed. Frank would have to do the jobs at a loss, but preserving his reputation was worth it.

Also in the customer service e-mail account, Frank found several notices from newhandshake.org. These notices indicated that complaints had been filed through the newhandshake.org button on the canvasbags.com home page. Frank had never received a complaint through that channel before, so he had to look up the login information from when he first signed up for newhandshake.org to be able to review the filings in his Resolution Center. There were five cases in the Resolution Center, two of which the customers had already closed and given Frank nonperformance strikes. The other three were still in progress, but the platform made clear that the customers were not happy and that they would soon close the case and give Frank more nonperformance strikes if he did not act quickly.

Frank recognized that all five of the customers who had reported complaints through the Resolution Center had already communicated with him via e-mail. One had agreed to cancel the order for a full refund, and the other four had jobs that were currently in progress. Over the next 24 hours, the three customers whose complaints were still in progress informed newhandshake.org that their concerns had been addressed by Frank's outreach and that they would like to close their complaints with no nonperformance strike against Frank. The other two cases that were already closed were a different matter. Frank contacted one of the consumers and asked if they would be willing to remove the strike now that Frank had returned and was addressing their issue. That consumer agreed to do so, and they logged in and requested removal through the newhandshake.org website. The last consumer, who had already received a full refund, did not respond to Frank's e-mails.

Frank decided to appeal the last strike. He logged into the Resolution Center, found the case in question, and clicked "appeal strike" in his action menu. A form appeared where he could submit all the information about the transaction in question. Frank explained the whole situation, and even uploaded the e-mail exchange with the buyer where he showed that he had provided a full refund. Frank hit submit and awaited a decision.

Two days later, Frank received an e-mail from the newhandshake.org administration team. They had reviewed his appeal and, based on the information submitted, granted it. The e-mail explained that the nonperformance strike would be removed from his record. Frank was greatly relieved because now his record was clean again.

Analysis

The newhandshake.org system is designed for merchants like Frank. Signing up to participate in the system is a way to signal good intentions to future customers, which gets you more demand and more purchases. Also, the sites that promote newhandshake.org participating businesses can also refer new customers. Frank never had any issues, so his participation in the system gave him benefits—arguably without any downside. In fact, Frank even forgot his login because his buyers never felt the need to use the system.

The system became relevant due to unforeseen circumstances. This is a common story for small sellers. Something happens (maybe a family crisis or a medical emergency) and it causes a disruption in the business. Fortunately, Frank found out about it in time to recover. He used the newhandshake.org system to make things right with his buyers and get things back on track. For the one buyer who did not respond to Frank's follow-up, the appeals process (which actually grants the first appeal automatically, although Frank did not know that) was able to help Frank get his reputation back on solid footing.

Nonetheless, one could argue that the newhandshake.org system was more trouble than it was worth for Frank. It allowed a rogue complainant to leave a negative strike even after compensation. Additionally, Frank had been doing his best to solve issues through direct communications with customers. However, the reality is that he did fall behind in his responses and the system helped him get back on track.

track. Furthermore, the rogue complainer also might be the type to complain on social media, so newhandshake.org at least allowed Frank a channel for defending his company's good name through a more reputable and monitored system.

Case 6: Recycling

Jonathan Seligman heads up the Consumer Response team at the Lancaster County Consumers Association (LCCA). One Monday, Jonathan comes into work at 8:30 a.m. and, like he does most mornings, immediately pops open the reporting dashboard in his LCCA Resolution Center. The reporting dashboard has been configured to show several graphs indicating the volume of new cases that have been filed within Lancaster County over the last day, week, month, and year. The reporting dashboard also indicates which merchants are involved in the new filings. On this morning, Jonathan sees that there has been a significant number of new cases filed against a single merchant, Green Cycles, over the past three days. From the website, Jonathan sees that Green Cycles sells refurbished bikes and bike parts, and that the store is affiliated with a local nonprofit that promotes bike riding for kids. It seems that 11 cases have been filed by consumers complaining that the purchase they had recently made from Green Cycles had not yet arrived, with six new cases arriving over the weekend. In clicking through the information submitted by the consumers, Jonathan notes that several consumers mention that their repeated e-mails to Green Cycles have garnered no response.

Jonathan reviews the information Green Cycles shared when they signed up to participate in the newhandshake.org platform. Jonathan sends a message to the specified e-mail address (support@greencycles.com) to try to determine what is going on, but he gets no response. Jonathan also discovers that the phone number provided just goes to voicemail. Jonathan suspects that the Green Cycles website is still running and taking orders, but for some reason they are not being fulfilled. This is leading to new purchases coming in from consumers but nothing happening on the back end to actually process the purchases.

Jonathan makes the decision to suspend the Green Cycles newhandshake.org account within his management portal. The New Handshake button on the Green Cycles home page immediately turns to a new status message, which indicates there is an issue with Green Cycles and that a review is ongoing.

Two days later, Jonathan notices that consumer complaints against Green Cycles are continuing to come in. Clearly, the updated status message on the New Handshake button is not enough to dissuade consumers from making new purchases. Jonathan considers contacting some of the affiliated local nonprofits that promote bike riding and who are listed on the site, but Jonathan is just too overworked and busy with other issues to get that involved in the matter. There is still no response to e-mails sent to the support address. There is a note in one of the cases that a consumer contacted one of the nonprofits and spoke to a volunteer named Stacy, who explained that the person they had hired to run the Green Cycles website had recently quit on short notice and left town without turning over any of the site passwords or credentials. Stacy had been trying to get access to the e-mail accounts and passwords for the Green Cycles storefront to try to shut it down, but she was still having difficulty.

Two weeks later, Jonathan visits the Green Cycles website address but the site no longer comes up. All that appears is a crudely made message that says this website no longer exists. Most of the complaints filed turn into strikes against the business as the consumers who filed the cases largely give up any hope of getting redress. Jonathan suspends Green Cycles from the newhandshake.org program and the Green Cycles profile page is updated to say that Green Cycles is now out of business.

Analysis

When a business is failing, it is kind of like landing a plane. One option is to turn things around, find a way to get back into the black, and restore profitability and growth—like pulling back on the stick and taking the plane back up into the clouds. The second is to find a way to end the business gracefully, by paying off all the debts and winding down orders with full notice so that no one walks away unhappy—essentially landing the plane gently on the runway. The third is to just give up as the plane spirals faster and faster toward the ground, leaving unhappy business partners and customers, all angry that they lost money—in essence, giving up and letting the plane crash.

The reality is that businesses fail. Sometimes, these failures are immediate and unexpected. A mechanism like newhandshake.org cannot ensure that every business failure will be a smooth landing instead of a fiery crash. Having the Resolution Center in place can provide early warnings about impending failures, but it cannot ensure those failures occur without incident.

Takeaways

Because there are hundreds of millions of transaction problems, it is easy to imagine many more consumer and merchant case studies that would illuminate other aspects of this proposed systems design. Although cases can be broadly grouped into categories and types, each individual matter has its own specific details. Additionally, as the system is brought live, scaled, and refined, it will be possible to create case studies based upon fact patterns drawn from real cases. Data regarding real cases will also help guide further system developments and improvements.

CHAPTER 11

What's Next

The New Handshake *is built upon technologies that are currently available. However, if the past is a reliable predictor of the future, we can be certain that powerful new technologies are right around the corner. In fact, this design may seem primitive in just a few years. Newer tools emerge and further change the way we use technology to interact with each other. In this chapter, we consider how these advances may change the* New Handshake *in the coming years.*

The design we present in this book is only the first iteration in an ongoing effort to realize the potential of cross-border, global consumer redress. As the volume of cases grows alongside the inevitable expansion of online commerce, new technologies and techniques will emerge that will make the system faster, fairer, and more effective. With the understanding that predicting the future is always a dicey proposition, let's examine a few of these possible innovations and improvements, acknowledging that we cannot guess all of the new capabilities (e.g., augmented reality, telepresence, virtual currencies) that may ultimately prove helpful over the coming years.

Human-Powered Resolutions

Many face-to-face dispute resolution experts may be surprised by the lack of human-powered dispute resolution services in the *New Handshake* systems design. This omission was intentional, but it is not intended to be permanent. Many attempts at building global consumer redress systems have been stymied by the vetting and management of human mediators and arbitrators. Ensuring that these human dispute resolution service providers are well trained, ethical, impartial, and fairly compensated is an enormous task at the scale of cases we are contemplating. Dispute resolution experts have also been caught in debates that presume human interaction is essential to any type of conflict resolution processes.

We are not proposing to do away with all human interaction in conflict resolution. It is not difficult to envision a system under which panels of qualified neutrals around the world are accessible to provide dispute resolution services to consumers and businesses using the same core infrastructure that powers the automated Resolution Centers. In fact, there are many online dispute resolution programs currently operating that rely on human neutrals to resolve complex matters, such as family disputes, insurance cases, property tax appeals, and workplace issues. This may occur in person, or simply through computer-mediated communications (CMC). Online arbitrations, for example, are already in existence and may offer the best value for those who seek to avoid the costs, time, and stress of face-to-face processes.

If a consumer and a merchant are unable to resolve the disagreement through technology-facilitated negotiation, human mediation and arbitration can be offered on an opt-in basis. Some parties may seek solace in this option if they feel it would assist them in crafting effective solutions. Parties could pay these neutrals directly, or costs may be covered by system-generated revenues. Human neutrals may also be available for higher dollar value cases or only for certain types of complex cases (e.g., counterfeits or fraud). These neutrals may be affiliated with a particular dispute resolution organization or public entity, which may provide its own funds to support training and technology tools. It is even conceivable that law students could act as neutrals for these programs in cooperation with a law school clinic and subject to state "student practice rules."

It is extremely likely that human-powered resolutions will be integrated into this system over time. However, the addition of human neutrals and external dispute resolution service providers does introduce new ethical obligations and ongoing management challenges. Continuously improving systems for video and audio conferencing, integrated directly into web browsers and mobile devices, may also make human-powered processes more effective, efficient, and scalable. However, even with the advanced technology, human neutrals must be continually monitored. It is imperative to ensure compliance with ethical and performance standards, and the architecture of the overall system must reinforce the specific capabilities and permissible roles these neutrals can play within the process. But eventually, much like ICANN's Uniform Domain Name Dispute Resolution Protocol (UDRP), a diverse set of human-powered dispute resolution organizations around the world can help to ensure that each case within the *New Handshake* system is able to get an appropriate and effective resolution. Indeed, ODR can help to finally deliver on Frank Sanders' concept of the "multi-door courthouse," which has long inspired the global dispute resolution community.

Additional Integrations

The *New Handshake* system will not exist within a bubble. There are already a wide variety of existing cross-border consumer resolution systems in operation, with varying levels of technological sophistication. The EU ODR platform noted previously governs the largest geographic area. But there are similar regional and national systems in use as well, such as Profeco's CONCILIANET in Mexico. Some of these smaller systems are truly innovative in their close integration with government agencies and enforcement activities. Additionally, there are other software platforms that are widely used to manage cases and resolve problems that are not usually considered ODR tools. For example, there are customer relationship management tools such as Salesforce, or Customer Service Ticketing platforms such as Zendesk.

In order to succeed, the *New Handshake* platform must operate seamlessly with these other systems. It must be easy to connect a Resolution Center to a customer service ticketing system, for example, to ensure that information is always synced up and the platforms are not working at cross-purposes. Although it appears daunting, it is clearly doable. Technologies exist to bring this to fruition.

The EU regulation requires that all EU merchants inform their customers about the availability of the EU's ODR platform. While enforcement of this requirement is still haphazard, compliance is expected to spread over time. One possible integration would be for merchants who opt into the *New Handshake* system to be automatically brought into compliance with the EU regulations. In order to achieve this, the *New Handshake* would need to be able to auto-escalate consumer filings into the EU's ODR filing form with a single click, meaning the information gathered would need to match the EU's own data architecture.

The *New Handshake* system would also need to be able to insert EU-approved messaging into the appropriate areas within the merchant's e-commerce and transaction systems. There might also be a path back from the EU platform into the *New Handshake* system. This would allow for one form-filing into two systems: one within the EU and one on a global level. This would be especially useful for EU purchasers or merchants transacting on a global level. Moreover, it is also possible that the *New Handshake* platform can be approved as a dispute resolution service provider under the EU rules and administer certain resolutions processes post-referral in addition to pre-referral. There is talk of EU-style ODR regulations being launched in other geographies (i.e., Russia and China), so the *New Handshake* system may provide easy compliance for merchants in those regions as well.

Certain business and trade associations may decide they want to integrate more closely with the *New Handshake* platform. Perhaps a Chamber of Commerce or a group of affiliated merchants (e.g., the Electronic Retailers Association) will decide that they want all of their members to opt into the *New Handshake* so as to underscore the trustworthiness of the industry. Maybe merchants who have had difficulties with bad buyer experiences in the past will be required to opt into the program so they have more effective tools for tracking and responding to issues reported by their consumers. The platform must be constructed in a way that makes it easy for these organizations to connect into the *New Handshake* system, perhaps by signing up a large group of merchants at once rather than submitting individual applications by hand.

Eventually, marketplaces and e-commerce storefronts may want to automate participation for all of their member merchants. For example, all the sellers who sign up for a global online marketplace may be automatically defaulted into membership, with the Resolution Center tools integrated directly into the marketplace platform. New merchants signing up for e-commerce storefronts may also get their own integrated Resolution Center by default, and *New Handshake* buttons will be included on their home pages without any additional steps required. For existing merchants already live in a particular platform, there may be *New Handshake* apps available as add-ons that make opting into the global redress system as simple as clicking "Install" and answering a few questions.

This ease of integration will take time to roll out across the major transaction platforms, but once achieved, it will be invaluable in expanding the reach of the system to as many consumers and merchants as possible. At conferences around the world, we continually lament the lack of integration and coordination among consumer claims processes. The current systems are a patchwork of unworkable systems. Consumers crave "one stop shopping" for filing claims and getting resolutions. Merchants also will save time and money working within an integrated system. Now is the time to begin the integration effort.

New Technologies

The frontier of online dispute resolution is always being pushed forward by innovations in technology. The earliest ODR experiments were dial-up, text-only, modem-based platforms with very limited communication options provided to participants. Over the next few years, ODR was enhanced by each new technological innovation, from the launch of the Internet, the launch of iPhone and Android devices, to free video conferencing services like Skype and Zoom, real-time joint document editing like Google Docs, and the expansion of social networks such as Facebook and LinkedIn.

Even offline innovations such as LCD projectors and digital cameras have proven quite useful for ODR. We can recall when law firms first integrated video conferencing for negotiations and mediations, and use of video proved powerful in courtrooms across the globe. The International Chamber of Commerce was on the cutting edge when it integrated technology into its arbitration center in Paris.

We cannot imagine what technologies await us in the coming years. However, we can be sure that these advances will continue to expand the scope and utility of ODR. Sometimes, the most heralded new technology quickly fizzles out (e.g., Google Glass) while a more useful technology sneaks in under the radar, slowly emerging into the public consciousness as it becomes more powerful (e.g., Amazon Echo). The idea of a device sitting on our desk, listening to a negotiation via a microphone and forming its own conclusions via natural language processing, is not that far off. Imagine if disputants can ask a small black box sitting on the desk listening to negotiations what it thinks would be fair, and get a technology-generated resolution proposal that the disputants can adopt, revise, or ignore. Voice-based services such as Siri, Echo, Alexa, and Cortana demonstrate that such a concept is no longer so far-fetched.

Artificial Intelligence

New technologies also relate to the use of artificial intelligence in the dispute resolution process. One of the most foundational concepts in ODR is the idea of the "fourth party." Originally introduced by Ethan Katsh and Janet Rifkin in their book *Online Dispute Resolution* (2001), the fourth party describes technology as another party sitting at the table, alongside party one and party two (the disputants) and the third party (the human neutral, such as a mediator or arbitrator).

The fourth party can play many different roles in a dispute. In most current ODR processes, the fourth party is largely administrative, handling tasks such as case filing, reporting on statistics, sharing data, and facilitating communications. However, the fourth party is capable of much more, and that capability is expanding as the power of computers expands. It is inevitable that at some point we will rely on the fourth party not only to assist us in administrative tasks but to help us resolve our issues, or maybe even to decide matters outright.

This phenomenon is often referred to as artificial intelligence, but in fact the concept of the fourth party stretches beyond traditional notions of artificial intelligence. An algorithm does not need to think like a human in order to effectively play the role of mediator or arbitrator. Sophisticated sets of rules and policies can be very effective in resolving fact-pattern-based cases, such as item-not-received disputes or even traffic cases. Case analysis tools can match likely solutions to incoming problems, perhaps initially only on an advisory basis. Technologies may surface key questions that the parties should address, or offer a library of suggested approaches the disputants can utilize if they like. Consider the aptitude for artificial intelligence to assist a Cortana-like device, as noted above, in suggesting possible solutions for parties' disputes—perhaps solutions that offer win-win outcomes when parties are at an impasse.

Technology platforms and sophisticated algorithms also hold great promise for addressing the implicit bias that infects face-to-face and human-controlled dispute resolution processes. Algorithms can be designed in such a way that they do not factor in external information that might bias outcomes, such as race, ethnicity, age, sex, or other factors that human decision makers are unable to ignore. Algorithms can also do a much better job providing consistent outcomes across thousands or millions of cases, working at a scale that human neutrals could never contemplate. Algorithms are also extremely cheap compared to human neutrals, perhaps resolving complex disputes over weeks and months for only a few pennies per case. It may feel oddly dehumanizing to contemplate these kinds of automated resolutions from our current vantage point, but it is far more conceivable than it was even a decade ago. A decade from now, the advantages may become so clear that it will seem oddly antiquated that we ever had hesitation about welcoming technology into our disputes in this way.

Once these fourth-party mechanisms become widely available, the *New Handshake* vision will become far more practical, affordable, and scalable. There are complex ethical and procedural questions about how these approaches should be deployed and monitored, but those questions are no more complex than the systems design challenges we have outlined over the course of this book. The algorithmic mediator and evaluator are not as far away as they might seem, and if deployed correctly, they will be a powerful asset in providing fast and fair resolutions to consumers around the globe.

In 1965, Gordon Moore, the co-founder of Intel, coined the phrase "Moore's Law," which projected that the number of transistors per square inch on integrated circuits would double every 18 months. This means that, when practically applied, the computing power of a microchip doubles about every two years. Moore's Law has held true ever since, even though some experts estimate it may top out in the next decade. However, this exponential growth curve has powered the modern information technology revolution. We now carry phones in our pockets that are thousands of times more powerful than the computers that NASA used to send a man to the moon. On the day that Apple launched the iPhone 7, they sold more transistors than had ever been made prior to the year 1995. These trends will not only continue, they will accelerate.

Futurist Ray Kurzweil uses the term "singularity" to describe a point in the future where the expansion of power in technologies such as computers, genetics, nanotechnology, robotics, and artificial intelligence will hit an inflection point that moves faster than our ability to understand what is going on. His current estimate puts this date around the year 2045. After that point, machine intelligence will vastly exceed all human intelligence combined. Eventually, we may rely on these super intelligent machines to do things we always believed only humans were capable of handling, like driving cars or writing books. It is no longer inconceivable to think that computers may one day drive our justice systems, both online and offline.

Preserving Human Connection

That is not to say that humans are or will be irrelevant in dispute resolution. Empathy, professionalism, wisdom, and judgment built on human interactions are invaluable. As an initial matter, humans remain at the core in creating ODR systems and devising the algorithms. Putting that aside, however, human interactions remains vital for certain cases. For example, criminal and constitutional cases remain the business of people-focused courtrooms. Moreover, there are sensitive issues than can only be addressed in person. Empathy transcends artificial intelligence. The power of personal apology has its place.

Furthermore, everyday disputes will continue to be resolved informally on-the-spot through human interactions. You may stop at a store's customer service desk to get an immediate price adjustment if you see that you were overcharged for the cookies you just bought. You will inevitably resolve many purchasing disputes at the store where you bought the item, and consolidated claims will continue to have a place in resolving safety-related issues. Moreover, disputes with neighbors and friends will usually be best solved in person.

Nonetheless, ODR has a vital role in e-commerce. We are talking about contracts formed over the Internet, and thus ODR seems natural for the parties who conclude these digital deals. ODR is tied to the fundamental dynamics of e-contracts and technological innovation. The expansion of technology has propelled e-contracts and will similarly drive the expansion of ODR. Yes, there will be many fits and starts, as technological innovation is never a straight line. It is never clear which technologies humans will embrace and which they will reject. However, understanding the inevitability of these forces can help us to shape future innovation in ODR and to ensure the continued relevance and efficacy of ODR over the longer term.

Conclusion

Our lives are moving online. The ubiquity of technology, accelerated by increasing power and decreasing costs, means that this trend will only accelerate. In the dawn of the digital age, we spent maybe 2 percent of our day connected to global networks, usually over a slow modem connection. Now, powerful wireless computers in our pockets take us closer to 30 or 40 percent. Soon, technology (maybe the Internet of Things, or Pokemon Go, or antennas stuck in our ears) will bring us as high as 80 to 90 percent. As a result, we are building a new society for ourselves in cyberspace, as evidenced by the movement of common consumer contracts from the in-person to the online world.

This migration is important for the resolution of e-commerce conflicts. Online interactions do not work the same way as face-to-face interactions. Time, place, and identity are all more fluid online, yet people are just as complicated online as they are in the face-to-face world. It may seem easy to automate contract formation, but those same contracts will inevitably fall victim to conflicts. For this new society, we must develop innovative social institutions to resolve conflicts just like we have developed in the offline world.

That is what *New Handshake* is about. In the offline world, we have traditionally relied on processes backed by social trust to fairly resolve problems. We have agreed to use these processes should something go wrong, and we once backed up that agreement with a handshake. We could rely on that symbol of trust to ensure the fairness of a deal. You could shake the hand of the farmer at the corn stand and rest assured that you could get replacement corn or your money back if the corn was full of worms.

Now we must create parallel processes to support our online interactions and our e-contracts. These processes cannot be tied to the same offline concepts of jurisdiction, location, and enforcement. Consumers making purchases online do not have the opportunity to look the merchant in the eye while concluding the deal. We therefore need to reach a new agreement to underscore social trust in the online world. The design presented in this book is a first attempt to envision how a system like that could work.

The justice system is inevitably being transformed by technology, but that change it not happening in a vacuum. It is happening because consumers, citizens, and disputants demand it. There is no question that this change will occur. The only question that remains is whether it will take 2, 5, or 10 years for these changes to fully play out. Once the justice system is transformed, online resolution of issues will become the new normal. It will not be controversial at all, or even seen as particularly innovative. We probably will not even remember how we used to resolve issues back in the Dark Age before technology was an option. We are quickly moving from the Dark Age to the Digital Age.

If online commerce is to continue to grow, consumers must be assured that they can work out any problems they encounter quickly and effectively. This is important not only for consumers and consumer advocates but for businesses as well. Businesses have bet billions of dollars on the expansion of e-commerce; as a result, business leaders increasingly recognize their responsibility to provide consumers fast and fair redress to any problems that arise. However, businesses are not simply providing this functionality to consumers out of the goodness of their hearts. Data analytics demonstrate clearly that the old zero-sum framings for the buyer-seller relationships are no longer appropriate. Businesses now must realize that they must provide effective redress out of self-interest because their future success is contingent upon the development of this social trust.

Make no mistake, there will be winners and losers from this transformation. However, if we design the system correctly, we can ensure that the businesses who step up to the plate and take care of their buyers will be rewarded. By contrast, the businesses who shirk their responsibilities and continue to take advantage of their power in business-to-consumer transactions will lose over the longer term.

Nonetheless, our enthusiasm for building these new dispute resolution mechanisms should not overshadow our focus on principles of justice and ethical judgment. Those concerns must remain paramount. Indeed, justice and fairness must be at the core of not only the design phase of the *New Handshake,* but also the ongoing evolution of these systems. Components mentioned earlier, such as transparency and external audits, will remain vital. This vision is not simply for another merchant-sponsored internal claims system or government website for voicing complaints. Those systems have their place and limitations in scope. Instead, we are proposing an idea for an integrated system that gives consumers a hub, and one-stop-shop, for getting help on their e-commerce claims.

The time is right to tackle this challenge. Global e-commerce requires a fast and fair resolution system, and most international organizations around the world now agree that ODR is the best way to power it. ODR is merely the latest iteration of Lex Mercatoria, or Merchant Law, which has provided the foundation of cross-border redress for more than a thousand years. The *New Handshake* is the extension of Lex Mercatoria into the consumer sphere. Technology has empowered consumers to transact internationally, opening opportunities for both businesses and consumers. It is obvious that technology must now create redress options for these transactions, much like international arbitration has created redress for cross-border commercial transactions for many years.

It may seem daunting to contemplate the scope of work required to make this design a reality. Changing consumer sentiment through the introduction of new ODR processes will not be easy. Litigation and general complaint sites are the comfortable norm, and consumer inertia is difficult to overcome. Consumers may fear the unknown and presume that businesses will always have an advantage in

ODR systems. Convincing merchants, NGOs, and consumer advocates around the world to launch this new system is no small task. However, consider how daunting it was for the pioneers who originally built the redress systems we currently rely upon in the offline world. This is an opportunity for us to craft institutions that will reinforce trust for generations to come. An opportunity like that does not come around very often.

This book was designed to begin the conversation, not end it. Now is the time for ODR systems designers, online merchants, payment providers, marketplace administrators, consumer advocates, lawyers, judges, students, and policy makers to work together to build the next generation of consumer protection. The design presented in this book is intended to be a launching point, not an ending point, for that effort.

More than a decade of work within international organizations has resulted in a global agreement that ODR is the best way to resolve e-commerce claims. It is the only way for us to transcend the difficulties and limitations of our current consumer protection systems and to develop something better. The degree of consensus around these points makes plain that the time is right to launch this new system. The Internet is enabling collaboration and transparency on an unprecedented scale, flattening the world and blurring borders. The tools and the will are converging to finally realize the potential of the Internet in empowering consumers and expanding access to justice. The window of opportunity is open, and a consensus is building across the public, private, and nonprofit sectors. Now it is up to us to act.

Bibliography

Primary Sources

Amy J. Schmitz, *Remedy Realities in Business to Consumer Contracting*, 58 ARIZONA L. REV. 213–61 (2016).

Amy J. Schmitz, *Access to Consumer Remedies in the Squeaky Wheel System*, 39 PEPPERDINE L. REV. 279–366 (2012).

Colin Rule, *Technology and the Future of Dispute Resolution*, DISPUTE RESOLUTION MAGAZINE (2015), http://www.colinrule.com/writing/drmag.pdf (last visited June 15, 2016).

Colin Rule, *Online Dispute Resolution for Business* (Jossey-Bass, 2002).

Ethan Katsh & Colin Rule, *What We Know and What We Need to Know About Online Dispute Resolution*, 67 S.C. L. REV. 329 (2016), http://www.americanbar.org/content/dam/aba/images/office_president/katsh_rule_whitepaper.pdf (last visited September 1, 2016).

Ethan Katsh & Janet Rifkin, *Online Dispute Resolution: Resolving Conflicts in Cyberspace* (Jossey-Bass, 2001).

Ethan Katsh, *Law in a Digital World* (Oxford University Press, 1995).

Ethan Katsh, Daniel Rainey & Mohamed Wahab eds., *Online Dispute Resolution: Theory and Practice* (Eleven International Publishers, 2012), http://www.ombuds.org/odrbook/Table_of_Contents.htm, last visited April 10, 2016.

Ethan Katsh, *Online Dispute Resolution: Some Implications for the Emergence of Law in Cyberspace,* 10(2) LEX ELECTRONICA 1, 6 (Winter 2006), http://www.lex-electronica.org/articles/v10-3/katsh.htm (last visited May 16, 2012).

Ethan Katsh, *The Electronic Media and the Transformation of Law* (Oxford University Press, 1989).

Larry Lessig, *Code and Other Laws of Cyberspace* (Basic Books, 1999).

Lucille M. Ponte, *Boosting Consumer Confidence in E-Business: Recommendations for Establishing Fair and Effective Dispute Resolution Programs for B2C Online Transactions*, 12 ALB. L.J. SCI. & TECH. 441, 443 n.3 (2002).

Pablo Cortes, *Online Dispute Resolution for Consumers in the European Union*. Routledge Research in Information Technology and E-Commerce Law (Routledge, 2010).

Richard Susskind, *The Future of Law: Facing the Challenges of Information Technology* (Clarendon Press, 1996).

Richard Susskind, *Tomorrow's Lawyers: An Introduction to Your Future* (Oxford University Press, 2013).

Richard Susskind & Daniel Susskind, *The Future of the Professions: How Technology Will Transform the Work of Human Experts* (Oxford University Press, 2015).

Chapter 1: Where We Are Now

Adi Ayal, *Harmful Freedom of Choice: Lessons from the Cellphone Market*, 74 LAW & CONTEMP. PROBS. 91, 91–100 (2011).

Alice F. Stuhlmacher & Amy E. Walters, *Gender Differences in Negotiation Outcome: A Meta-Analysis*, 52 PERSONNEL PSYCHOL. 653, 656 (1999).

Alice F. Stuhlmacher et al., *Gender Difference in Virtual Negotiation: Theory and Research*, 57 SEX ROLES 329, 334–36 (2007).

Amy J. Schmitz, *Access to Consumer Remedies in the Squeaky Wheel System*, 39 PEPP. L. REV. 2, 313 (2012) (quoting Arthur Best & Alan R. Andreasen, *Consumer Response to Unsatisfactory Purchases: A Survey of Perceiving Defects, Voicing Complaints, and Obtaining Redress*, 11 LAW & SOC'Y REV. 701, 723 (1977)).

Bård Tronvoll, *Complainer Characteristics When Exit Is Closed*, 18 INT'L J. SERV. INDUSTRY MGMT. 25, 25–51 (2007), available at www.emeraldinsight.com/0956-4233.htm.

Charles B. Craver & David W. Barnes, *Gender, Risk Taking, and Negotiation Performance*, 5 MICH. J. GENDER & L. 299, 309–10 (1999).

Consumer Financial Protection Agency Act, H.R. 3126, 111th Cong. §§ 111(a), 134(a) (2009).

Consumer Financial Protection Bureau, *About us*, http://www.consumerfinance.gov/the-bureau (last visited January 1, 2014).

Consumer Financial Protection Bureau, *CFPB and DOJ Order Ally to Pay $80 Million to Consumers Harmed by Discriminatory Auto Loan Pricing* (Dec. 20, 2013) http://www.consumerfinance.gov/newsroom/cfpb-and-doj-order-ally-to-pay-80-million-to-consumers-harmed-by-discriminatory-auto-loan-pricing (noting that the Equal Credit Opportunity Act prohibits "creditors from discriminating against loan applicants in credit transactions on the basis of characteristics such as race and national origin").

David Hill Koysza, *Preventing Defendants from Mooting Class Actions by Picking Off Named Plaintiffs*, 53 DUKE L.J. 781, 789 (2003).

Debra Pogrund Star & Jessica M. Choplin, *A Cognitive and Social Psychological Analysis of Disclosure Laws and Call for Mortgage Counseling to Prevent Predatory Lending*, 16 PSYCHOL. PUB. POL'Y & L. 85, 98–99 (2010).

Devon W. Carbado & Mitu Gulati, *Conversations at Work*, 79 OR. L. REV. 103, 108–10 (2000).

Dodd-Frank Wall Street Reform and Consumer Protection Act, PUB. L. NO. 111–203, 124 Stat. 1376 (2010) (codified in scattered sections of the U.S. Code).

Eugene J. Kelley, Jr. et al., *Offers of Judgment in Class Action Cases: Do Defendants Have a Secret Weapon?*, 54 CONSUMER FIN. L. Q. REP. 283 (2000).

Federal Communications Commission (FCC), *FCC Proposes $5.2 Million Fine Against U.S. Telecom Long Distance, Inc. for Deceptive Slamming, Cramming, and Billing Practices* (Jan. 24, 2014) http://www.fcc.gov/document/fcc-proposes-52-m-fine-against-us-telecom-long-distance-inc.

Frank E.A. Sander & Lukasz Rozdeiczer, *Matching Cases and Dispute Resolution Procedures: Detailed Analysis Leading to a Mediation-Centered Approach*, 11 HARV. NEGOT. L. REV. 1, 14 (2006).

Geraldine Szott Moohr, *Opting In or Opting Out: The New Legal Process or Arbitration*, 77 WASH. U. L.Q. 1087, 1093–97 (1999).

Jeffrey I. Shinder, *In Praise of Class Actions*, NAT'L L.J. at 39 (April 5, 2010).

Jeremy B. Merrill, *One-Third of Top Websites Restrict Customers' Right to Sue*, N.Y. TIMES (Oct. 23, 2014), http://www.nytimes.com/2014/10/23/upshot/one-third-of-top-websites-restrict-customers-right-to-sue.html (last visited Nov. 24, 2014).

Larry Bates, *Administrative Regulation of Terms in Form Contracts: A Comparative Analysis of Consumer Protection*, 16 EMORY INT'L L. REV. 1, 29–33 (2002).

Laurie A. Rudman, *Self-Promotion as a Risk Factor for Women: The Costs and Benefits of Counterstereotypical Impression Management*, 74 J. OF PERSONALITY & SOC. PSYCHOL. 629, 629–30 (1998).

Linda Babcock & Sara Laschever, *Women Don't Ask: Negotiation and the Gender Divide*, 20 (2003).

Lois Beckett, *Everything We Know About What Data Brokers Know About You*, PROPUBLICA (March 7, 2013) http://www.propublica.org/article/everything-we-know-about-what-data-brokers-know-about-you (last visited August 19, 2013).

Marco B.M. Loos, *Individual Private Enforcement of Consumer Rights in Civil Courts in Europe,* 5–14 (Ctr. for the Study of Eur. Contract Law Working Paper Series, Paper No. 2010/01), available at http://ssrn.com/abstract=1535819.

Matt Brownell, *Credit Card Chargebacks: Your Secret Weapon in Merchant Disputes*, DAILY FINANCE (Jul. 31, 2012), http://www.dailyfinance.com/2012/07/31/credit-card-chargeback-merchant-disputes.

Omri Ben-Shahar & Carl E. Schneider, *The Failure of Mandated Disclosure* 7–20, 40–55 (Chi. Law Sch. John M. Olin Law & Econ. Working Paper, 2d Series, Paper No. 516, 2010), available at http://www.law.uchicago.edu/files/file/516-obs-disclosure.pdf.

Oren Bar-Gill & Elizabeth Warren, *Making Credit Safer*, 157 U. PA. L. REV. 1, 22 (2008).

Oren Bar-Gill & Rebecca Stone, *Mobile Misperceptions*, 23 Harv. J.L. & Tech. 49, 118 (2009).

Peter B. Rutledge & Anna W. Howard, *Arbitrating Disputes Between Companies and Individuals: Lessons from Abroad*, 65 Disp. Resol. J. 30, 33 (2010).

Richard A. Posner, *Economic Analysis of Law* 3–28, Aspen Publishers; 7th ed. (February 7, 2007).

Richard A. Posner, *Rational Choice, Behavioral Economics, and the Law*, 50 Stan. L. Rev. 1551, 1559–75 (1998).

Russell Korobkin, *Bounded Rationality, Standard Form Contracts, and Unconscionability*, 70 U. Chi. L. Rev. 1203, 1204–06, 1222–25, 1243–44 (2003).

Russell Korobkin, *Symposium, Inertia and Preference in Contract Negotiation: The Psychological Power of Default Rules and Form Terms*, 51 Vand. L. Rev. 1583, 1605–09, 1627 (1998).

Shmuel I. Becher, *Behavioral Science and Consumer Standard Form Contracts*, 68 La. L. Rev. 117, 122–24 (2007).

U.S. Gov't Accountability Office, Gao-10-518, *Factors Affecting the Financial Literacy of Individuals with Limited English Proficiency* 1, 9–10 (2010), available at http://www.gao.gov/new.items/d10518.pdf.

William H. Redmond, *Consumer Rationality and Consumer Sovereignty*, 58 Rev. Soc. Econ. 177 (2000).

Wolf J. Rinke, *Don't Oil the Squeaky Wheel: And 19 Other Contrarian Ways to Improve Your Leadership Effectiveness* 133–38 (2004).

Chapter 2: What Consumers Want

Amy J. Schmitz, *Introducing the "New Handshake" to Expand Remedies and Revive Responsibility in ECommerce*, 26 University of St. Thomas L. Rev. 522–50 (2014).

Amy J. Schmitz, *Ensuring Remedies to Cure Cramming*, 14 Cardozo J. of Conflict Resolution 877–97 (2013).

Amy J. Schmitz, *Building Bridges to Consumer Remedies in eConflicts*, 34.4 U. A. L. Rev. 779, 779–95 (2012).

Consumer Reports, *Iffy Product? Now a Way to Tell* (Feb. 2011), available at http://www.consumerreports.org/cro/magazine-archive/2011/february/recalls-and-safety-alerts/iffy-product/index.htm.

Consumer Reports, *New Ways to Complain*, http://www.consumerreports.org/cro/money/consumer-protection/new-ways-to-complain/overview/index.htm (last visited January 12, 2015).

Consumer Reports, *Trouble with Recalls* (Feb. 2011), http://www.consumerreports.org/cro/magazine-archive/2011/february/home-garden/bad-products/recalls/index.htm.

Consumer Reports: Money Advisor, *No More Fine-Print Surprises* at 2 (Feb. 2011) (noting survey results).

NBC 9News, *How to Get What You Want from Customer Service* (July 16, 2014), interviewing Prof. Amy J. Schmitz, http://www.9news.com/story/money/business/2014/07/16/tips-for-getting-what-you-want-from-customer-service/12765815/.

Ian Ayres, *Fair Driving: Gender and Race Discrimination in Retail Car Negotiations,* 104 Harv. L. Rev. 817, 819–43 (1991).

Joseph Conlin, *The New Media and Marketing Landscape,* available at http://www1bpt.bridgeport.edu/~jconlin/InternetMarketing.pdf (last visited July 28, 2013).

Joshua Klayman & Young-Won Ha, *Confirmation, Disconfirmation, and Information in Hypothesis Testing,* 94 Psychol. Rev. 211 (1987).

Kristina Knight, *Online Shopping Expectations Are Rising,* available at http://www.bizreport.com/2008/01/online_shopping_expectations_are_rising.html (last visited May 16, 2012).

Matthew Dixon & Brent Adamson, *The Challenger Sale: Taking Control of the Customer Conversation* (Portfolio/Penguin, 2011).

Matthew Dixon, Brent Adamson, Pat Spenner & Nick Toman, *The Challenger Customer: Selling to the Hidden Influencer Who Can Multiply Your Results* (Portfolio/Penguin, 2015).

Matthew Dixon, Karen Freeman & Nicholas Toman, *Stop Trying to Delight Your Customers,* Harvard Bus. Rev. (July–August 2010), available at https://hbr.org/2010/07/stop-trying-to-delight-your-customers/ar/1 (last visited January 23, 2016).

Morris B. Holbrook & Elizabeth C. Hirschman, *The Experiential Aspects of Consumption: Consumer Fantasies, Feelings, and Fun,* 9 J. Consumer Res. 132 (1982).

Sharane Gott, *BBB Offers Tips on When and How to File a Complaint* (Apr. 24, 2013), http://www.bbb.org/blog/2013/04/bbb-offers-tips-on-when-and-how-to-file-a-complaint/, [http://perma.cc/6K8F-P4SX].

Tibbett L. Speer, *They Complain Because They Care,* 18 Am. Demographics 13 (1996) (noting "grousers are likely to remain loyal" if they are happy with resolution of their complaints).

Chapter 3: Lessons Learned on eBay

Amazon Web Services, *Amazon.com Price vs. eBay Price,* available at http://node_charts_production.s3.amazonaws.com/56fd95dfec274958c3f229941cf676a7.png (last visited May 16, 2012).

Colin Rule, *Making Peace on eBay: Resolving Disputes in the World's Largest Marketplace,* ACResolution Magazine (Fall 2008), available at http://colinrule.com/writing/acr2008.pdf (last visited June 15, 2016).

Henry Blodget, *Amazon Is Still Eating eBay's Lunch*, BUSINESS INSIDER, http://articles.businessinsider.com/2010-01-15/tech/30086371_1_powersellers-ebay-share (last visited May 16, 2012).

Rob Enderle, *EBay vs. Amazon: An Interesting Lesson in Customer Care*, available at http://www.itbusinessedge.com/cm/blogs/enderle/ebay-vs-amazon-an-interesting-lesson-in-customer-care/?cs=49557&page=2 (last visited May 16, 2012).

Chapter 4: The Business Case for Resolutions

Colin Rule, *Quantifying the Economic Benefits of Effective Redress: Large E-Commerce Data Seta and the Cost-Benefit Case for Investing in Dispute Resolution,* UNIV. OF ARKANSAS LAW REV. 2012, available at http://www.colinrule.com/writing/UALR2012.pdf (last visited June 10, 2016).

Pete Blackshaw, *Satisfied Customers Tell Three Friends, Angry Customers Tell 3,000: Running a Business in Today's Consumer-Driven World*, 4–6, Crown Business; 1st edition (July 8, 2008).

Chapter 6: Ethical Considerations

ABA/SPIDR/AAA, *Model Standards of Conduct for Mediators*, available at https://adr.org/aaa/ShowPDF?doc=ADRSTG_010409 (last visited December 6, 2015).

Colin Rule et al., *Virtual Virtues: Ethical Considerations for Online Dispute Resolution (ODR) Practice*, DISP. RESOL. MAG. (Fall 2010), available at http://colinrule.com/writing/virtualvirtues.pdf (last visited December 6, 2015).

Daniel Rainey, *Third-Party Ethics in the Age of the Fourth Party,* 1 INT'L J. DISP. RESOL. 37, 56 (2014).

ICANN, *Online Dispute Resolution Standards of Practice,* https://www.icann.org/en/system/files/files/odr-standards-of-practice-en.pdf (last visited December 6, 2015).

Ruha Devanesan & Jeffrey Aresty, *ODR and Justice—An Evaluation of Online Dispute Resolution's Interplay with Traditional Theories of Justice*, in ONLINE DISPUTE RESOLUTION: THEORY AND PRACTICE (Ethan Katsh, Daniel Rainey & Mohamed Wahab eds., 2012), available at http://www.ombuds.org/odrbook/devanesan_aresty.pdf (last visited December 16, 2015).

Chapter 7: Envisioning a Global Redress System

Colin Rule et al., *Designing a Global Consumer Online Dispute Resolution (ODR) System for Cross-Border Small Value-High Volume Claims—OAS Developments*, 42 UCC L. J. 221 (2010), available at http://colinrule.com/writing/ucclj.pdf, [http://perma.cc/SEV4-SDHD].

David J. Bilinsky, *10 Collaborative Principles for Leading a Successful ODR System Initiative*, ODR & CONSUMERS 2010 (Sept. 1, 2010), http://www.odrandconsumers2010.org/2010/09/01/10-collaborative-principles-for-leading-a-successful-odr-system-initiative.

Jelle van Veenen, *From :-(to :-): Using Online Communication to Improve Dispute Resolution* (Tilburg Inst. for Interdisciplinary Studies of Civil Law & Conflict Resolution Sys., Working Paper No. 002/2010, 2010), available at http://ssrn.com/abstract=1618719.

Lenden Webb, *Brainstorming Meets Online Dispute Resolution*, 15 AM. REV. INT'L ARB. 337, 357–58 (2004).

Lou Del Duca, Colin Rule & Brian Cressman, *Lessons and Best Practices for Designers of Fast Track, Low Value, High Volume Global eCommerce ODR Systems*, 6 Y.B.ARB. & MEDIATION 204 (2014), available at http://www.colinrule.com/writing/ebaydd.pdf (last visited June 15, 2016).

Vikki Rogers, Lou Del Duca & Colin Rule, *Designing a Global Consumer Online Dispute Resolution (ODR) System for Cross-Border Small Value-High Volume Claims–OAS Developments*, 42 UNIFORM COMMERCIAL CODE LAW J. 3, available at http://colinrule.com/writing/ucclj.pdf (last visited June 16, 2016).

Chapter 11: What's Next

Anjanette H. Raymond & Scott J. Shackelford., *Technology, Ethics, and Access to Justice: Should an Algorithm Be Deciding Your Case?*, MICH. J. INT'L L. 486, 492 (Spring 2014).

Chittu Nagarajan & Colin Rule, *Crowdsourcing Dispute Resolution Over Mobile Devices*, in MOBILE TECHNOLOGIES FOR CONFLICT MANAGEMENT: ONLINE DISPUTE RESOLUTION, GOVERNANCE, PARTICIPATION (2011), available at http://colinrule.com/ writing/mobile.pdf (last visited June 10, 2016).

Chittu Nagarajan & Colin Rule, *Leveraging the Wisdom of Crowds: The eBay Community Court and the Future of Online Dispute Resolution*, in ACRESOLUTION MAGAZINE (Winter 2010), available at http://colinrule.com/writing/acr2010.pdf (last visited June 15, 2016).

Frank E.A. Sander, *The Future of ADR—The Earl F. Nelson Memorial Lecture*, 2000 J. DISP. RESOL. 3, 5–6 (2000).

Geoffrey Davies, *Can Dispute Resolution Be Made Generally Available?*, 12 OTAGO L. REV. 305, 308–16 (2010).

Index

O

P

R

S

T

U

V

W

Y